Down East Christmas
Stained Glass Patterns

*55 pages of Holiday Themed
Stained Glass Patterns*

ISBN: 978-1-326-17473-6

*Gary Somers
©2025*

Easy Christmas Bells

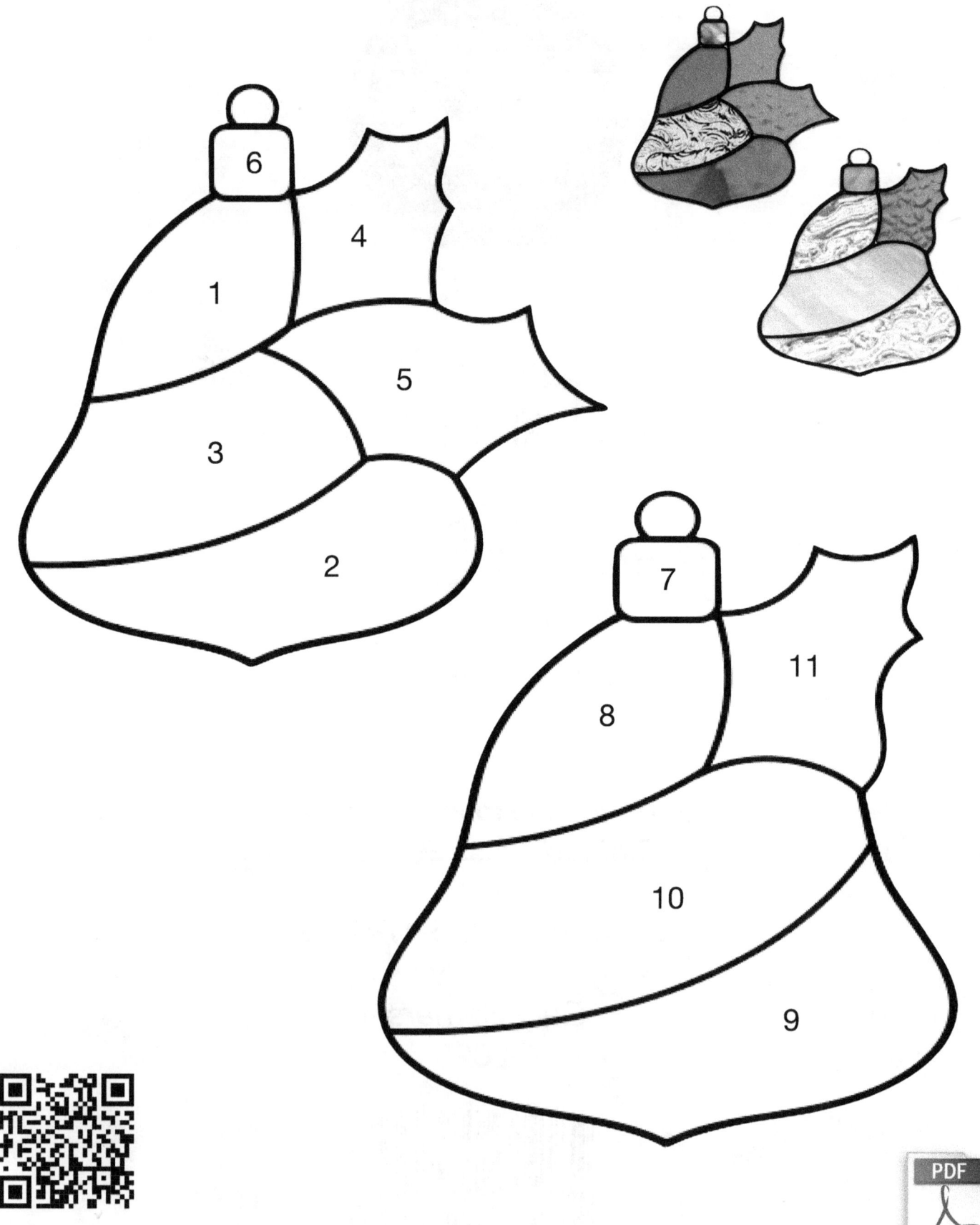

Down East Stained Glass

Candy Cane Christmas Tree

6 1/2" x 7 1/4"

Down East Stained Glass

Christmas Ornaments 4

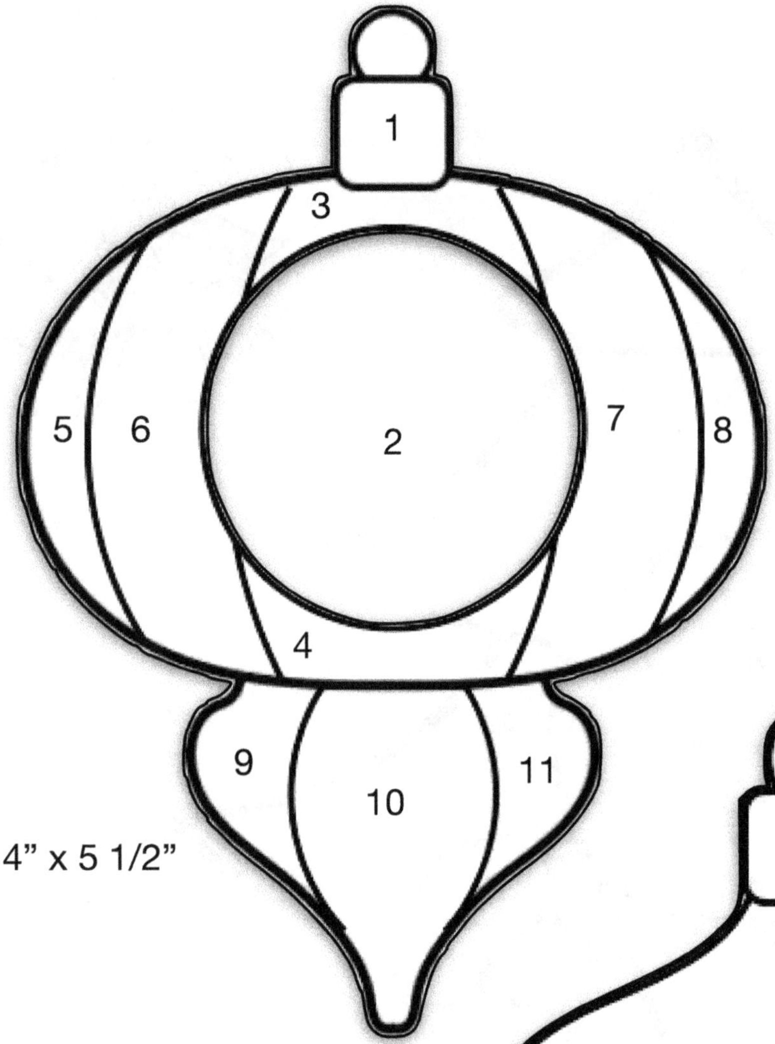

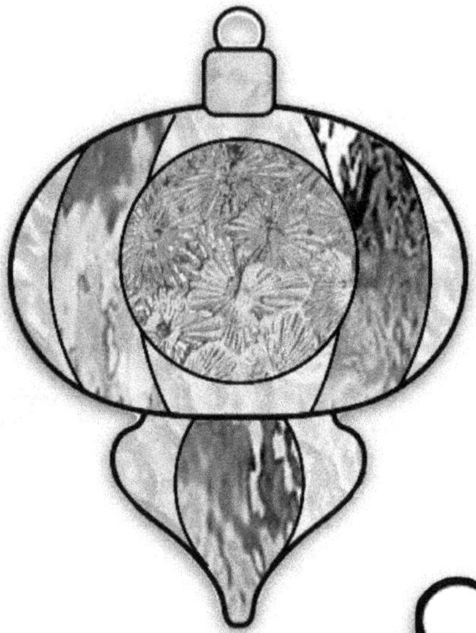

4" x 5 1/2"

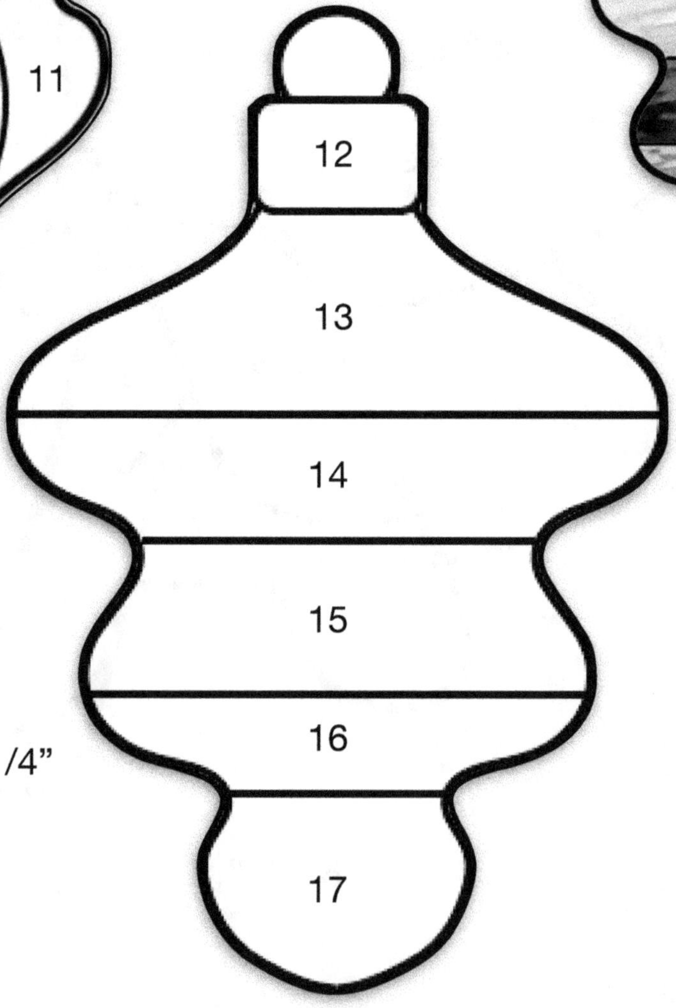

3 1/2" x 5 1/4"

Down East Stained Glass

Christmas Abstract Gnome Ornament

3 1/2" x 7"

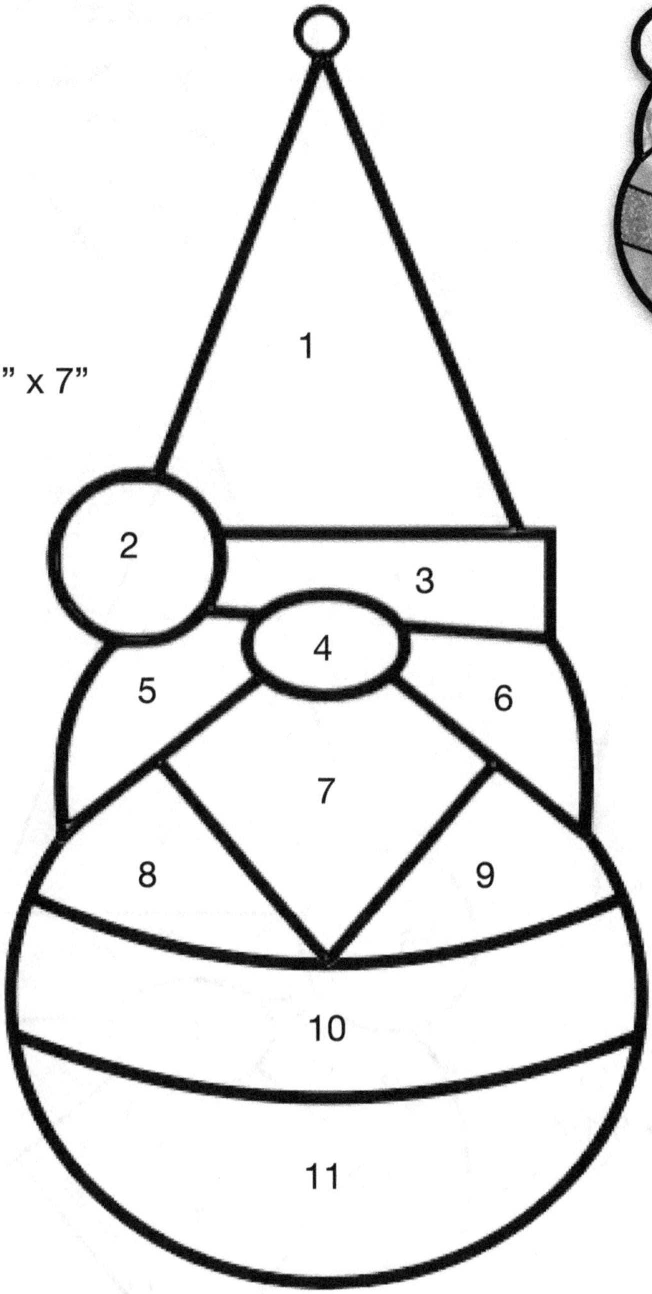

3" x 6"

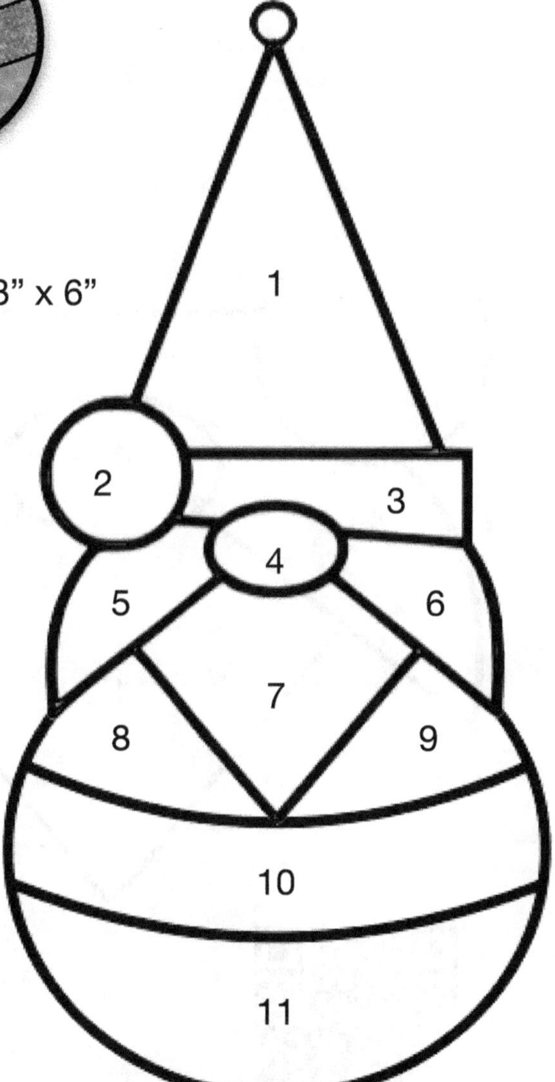

Down East Stained Glass

Christmas Abstract Gnome

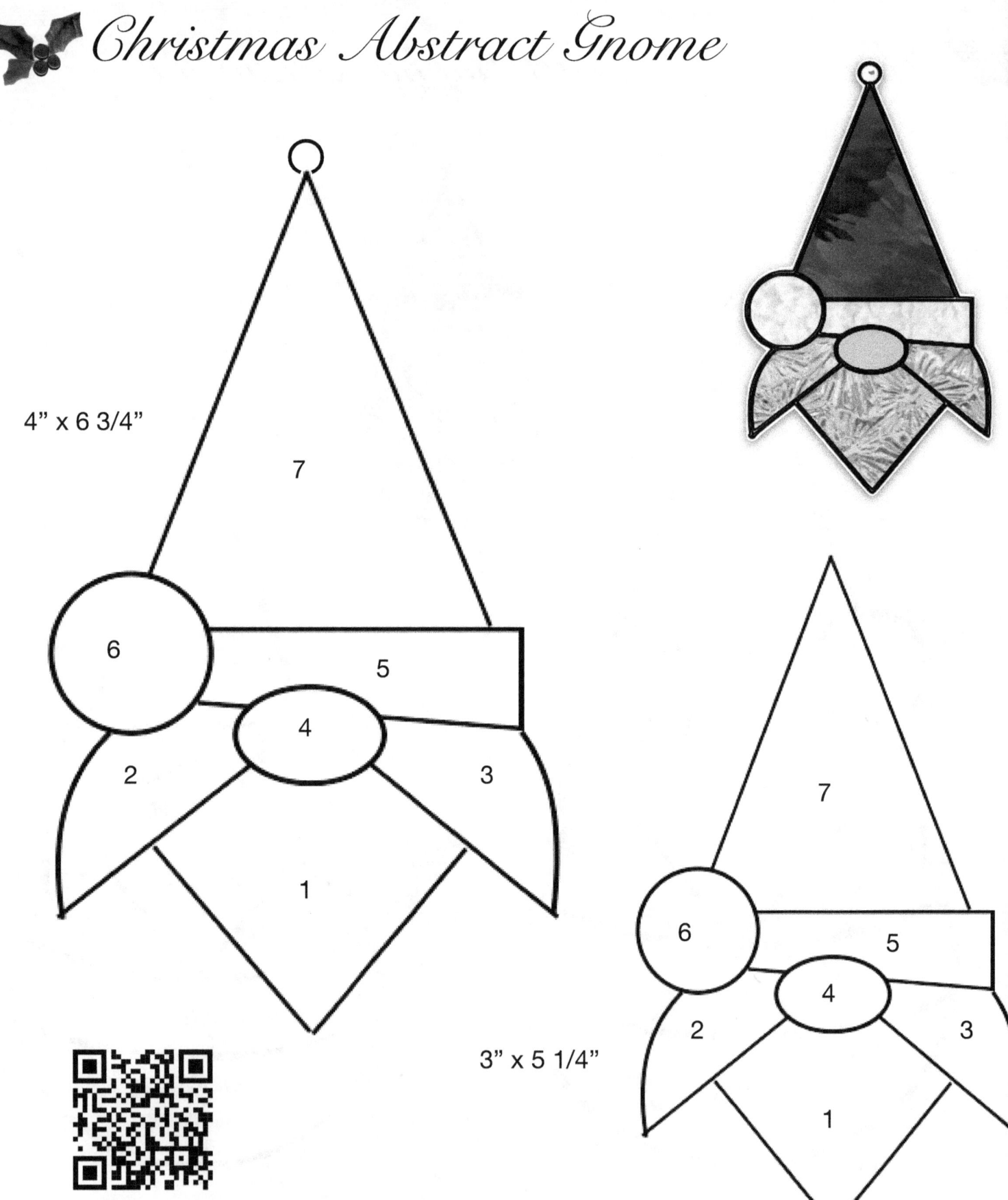

4" x 6 3/4"

3" x 5 1/4"

Down East Stained Glass

Christmas Bell Teardrop

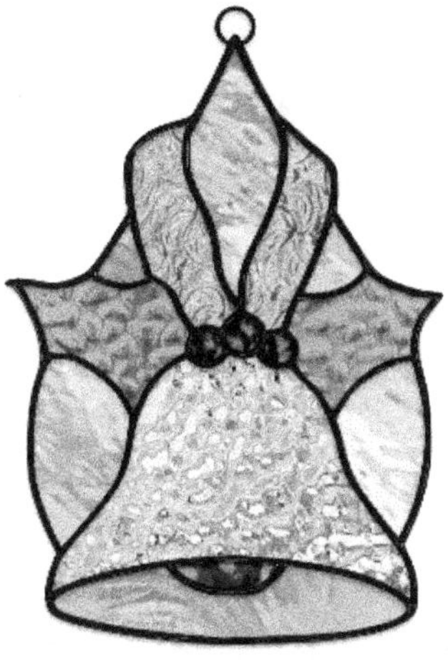

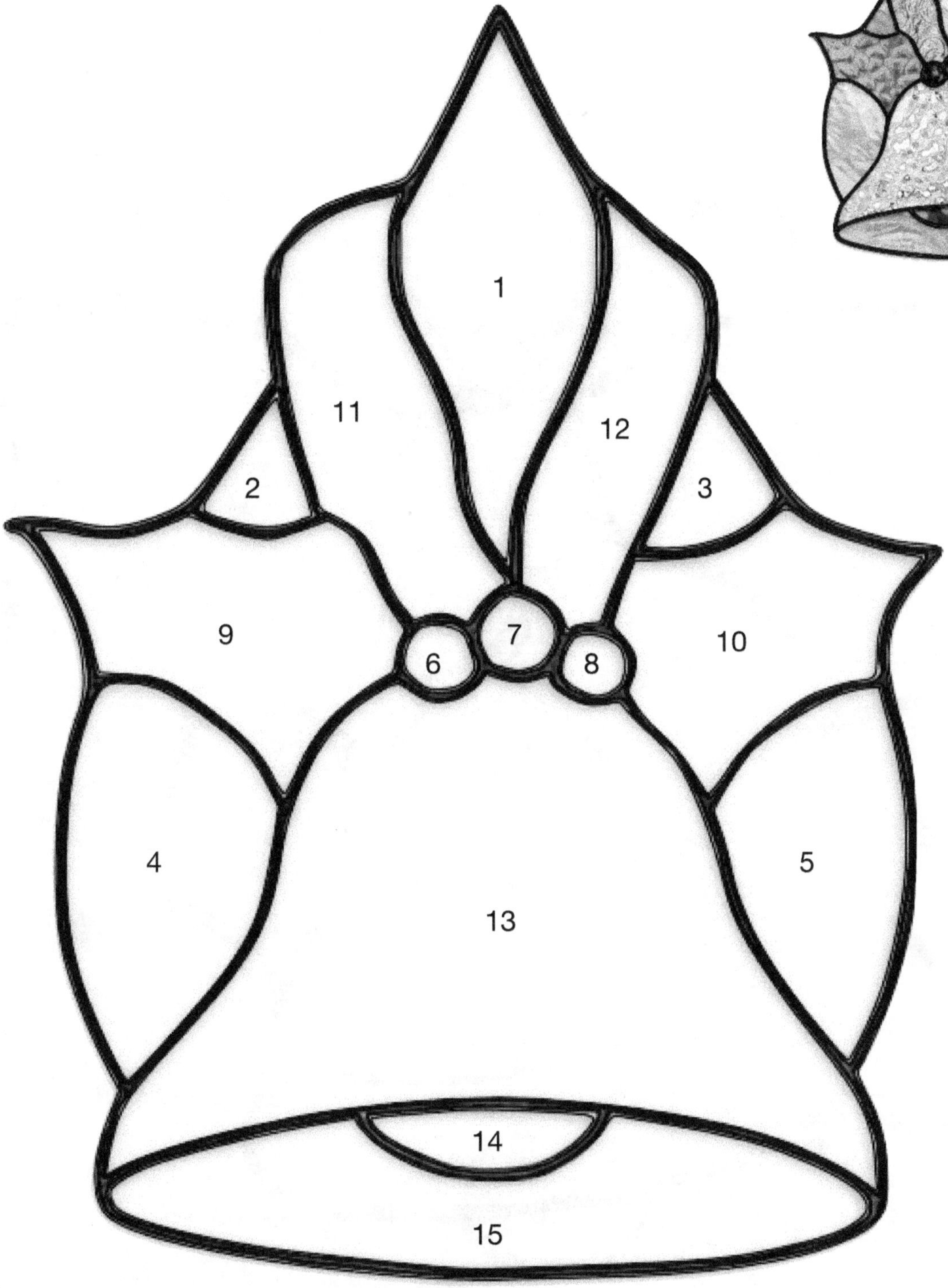

5 1/2" x 7 1/2"

Down East Stained Glass

Holy Spirit Ornament
2 sizes

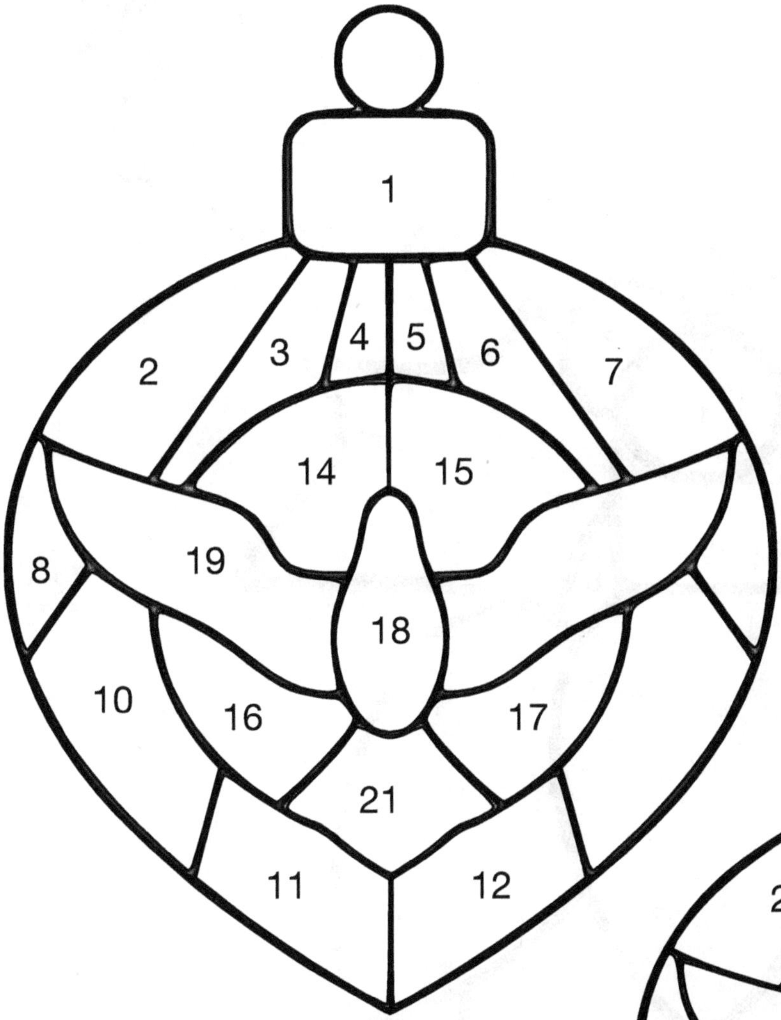

4" x 4 3/4"

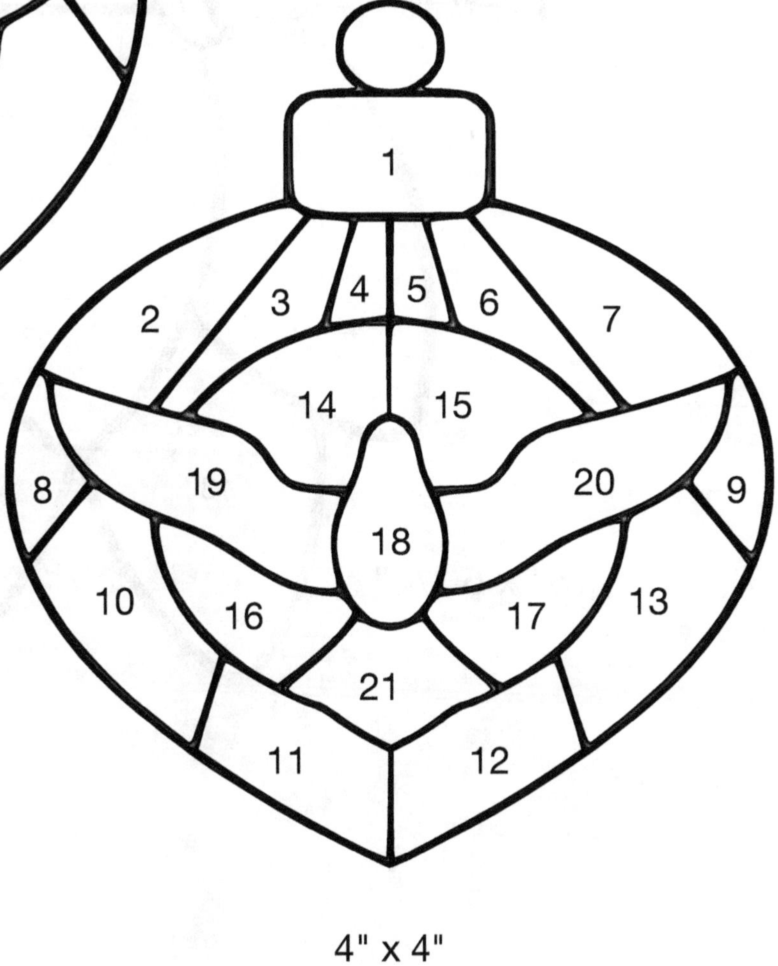

4" x 4"

Down East Stained Glass

Christmas Bulb Bouquet
2 sizes

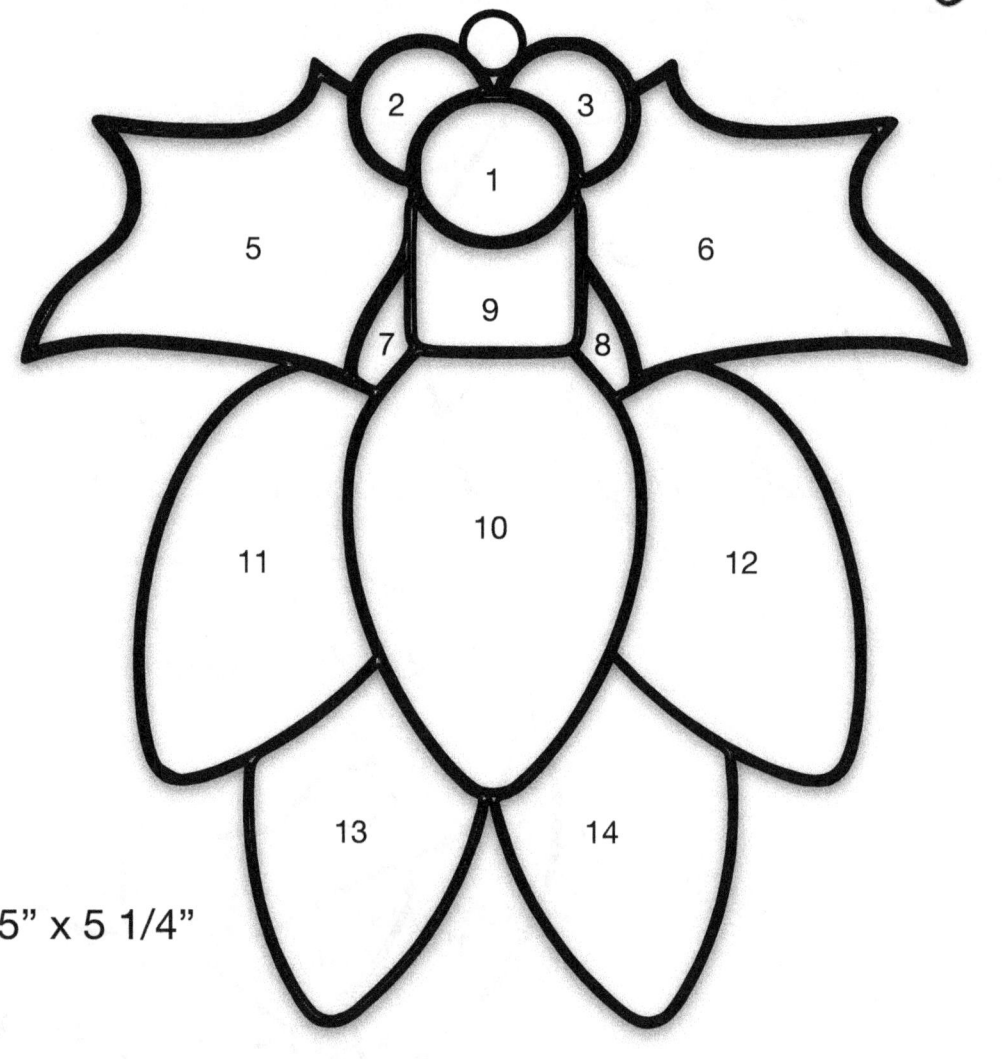

5" x 5 1/4"

Down East Stained Glass

Christmas Gnome Ornament 2
2 sizes

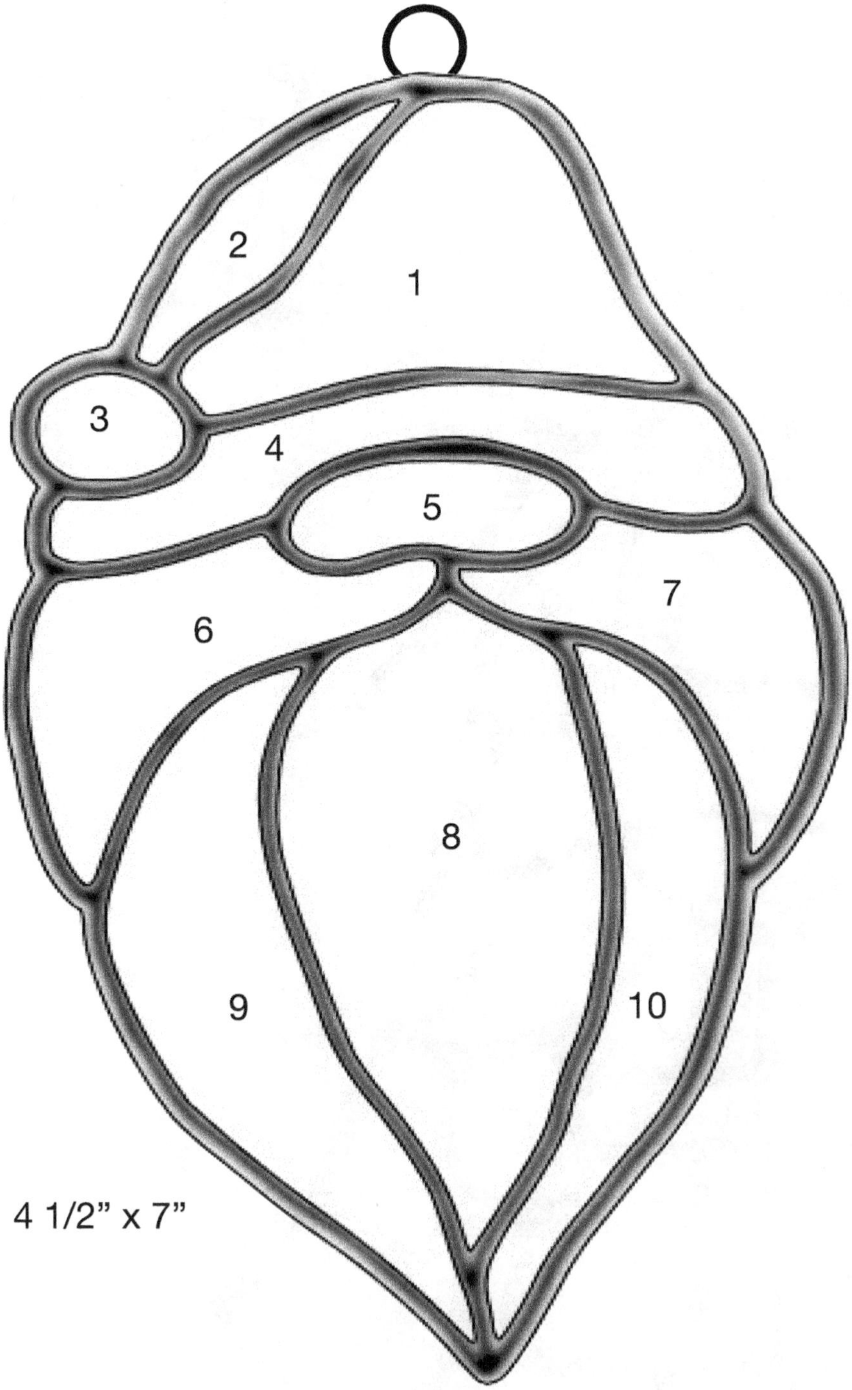

4 1/2" x 7"

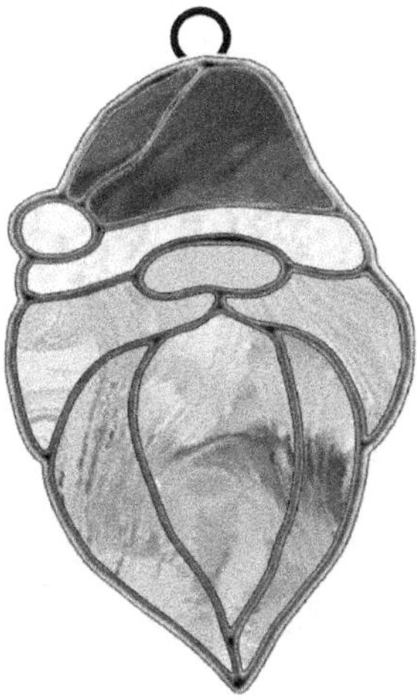

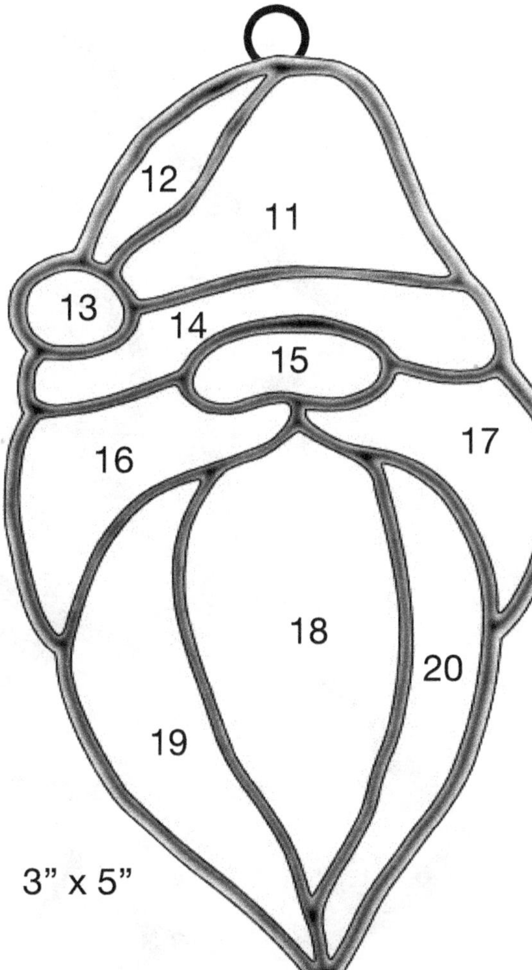

3" x 5"

Down East Stained Glass

Christmas Gnome
6" x 6 1/2"

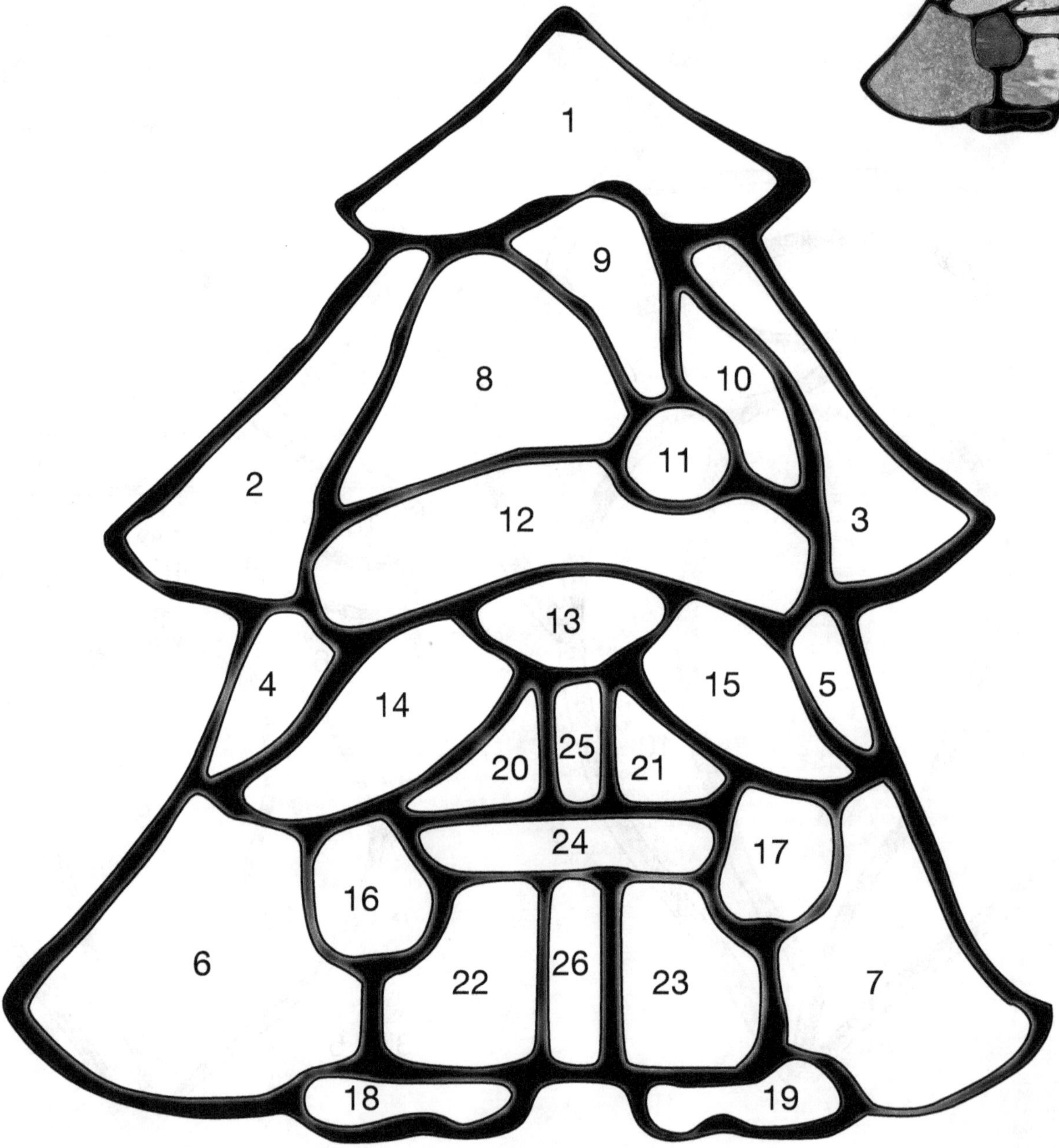

Down East Stained Glass

Christmas Holly Ornament

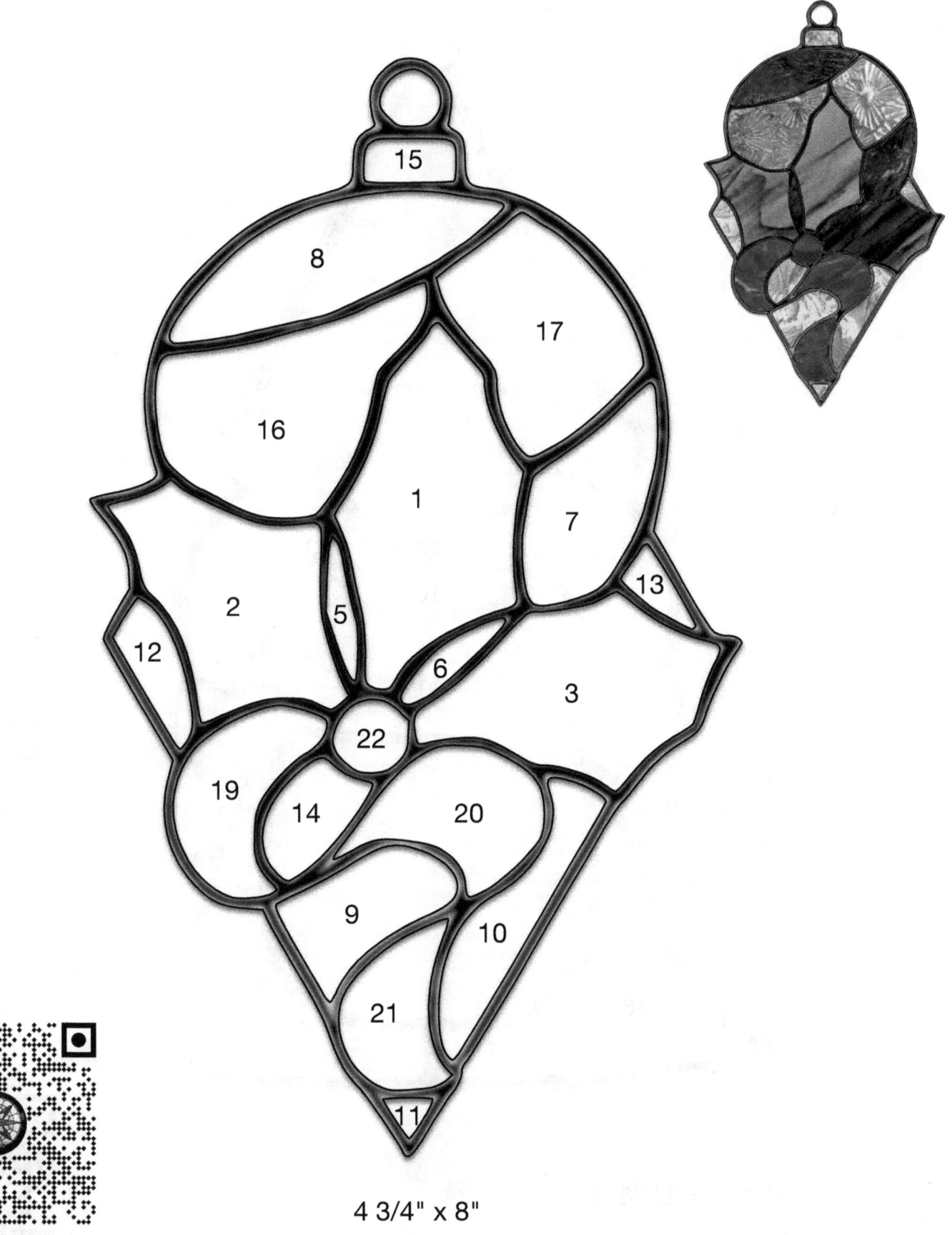

4 3/4" x 8"

Down East Stained Glass

 *Christmas Lady Gnome*

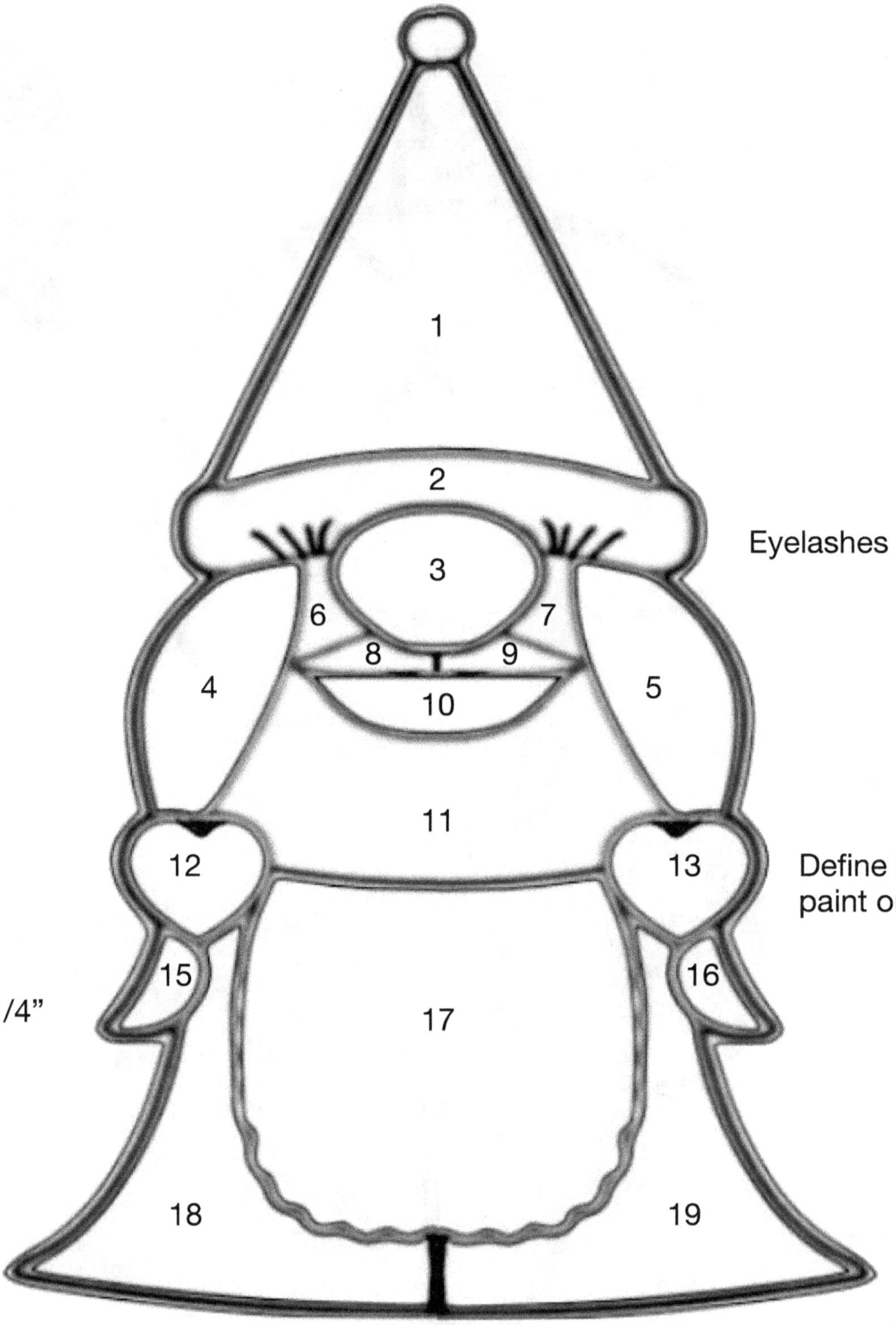

Eyelashes paint or wire

Define heart tops with paint or foil overlay

5 1/2" x 8 1/4"

Down East Stained Glass

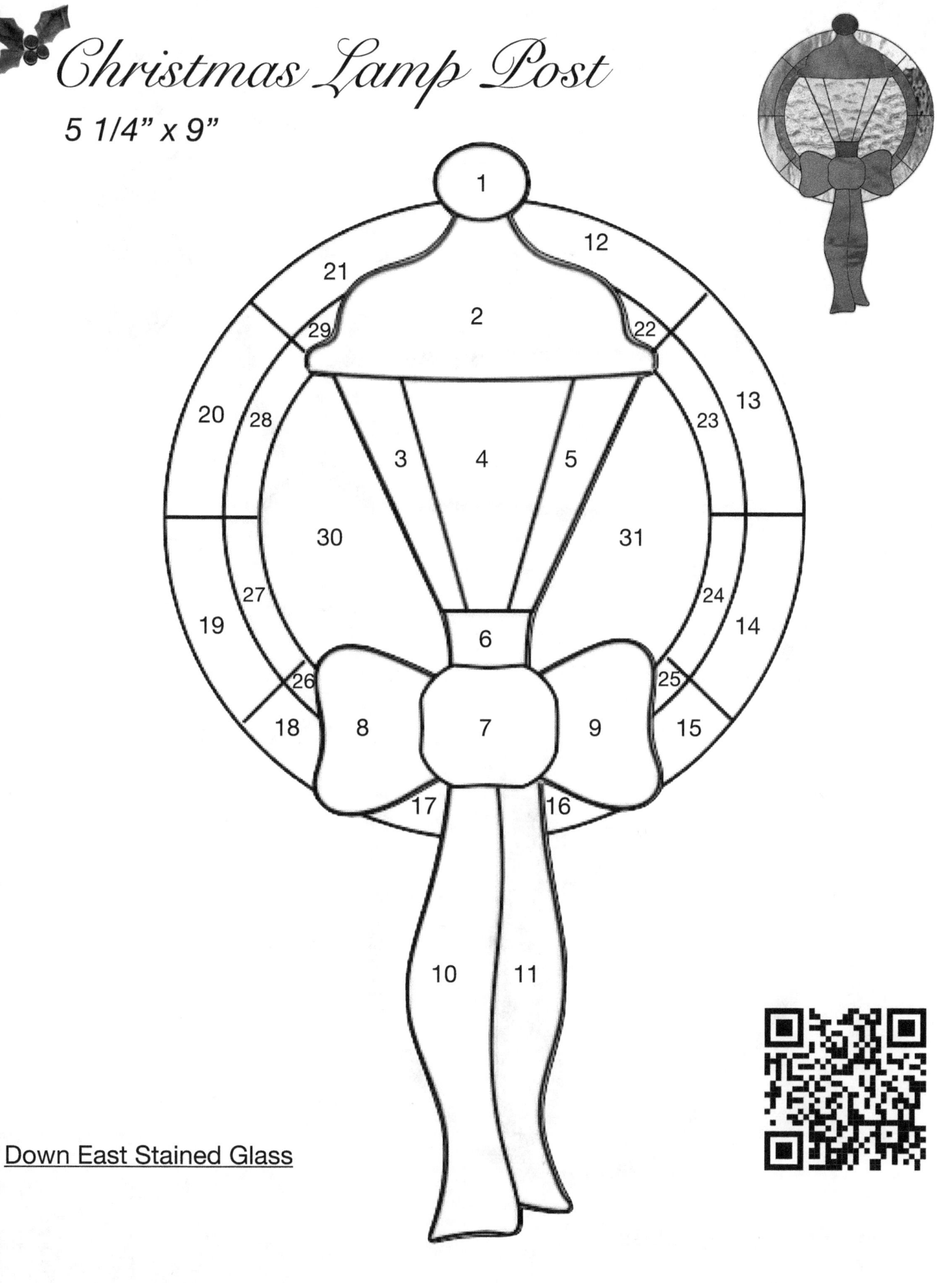

Christmas Lobster Claw

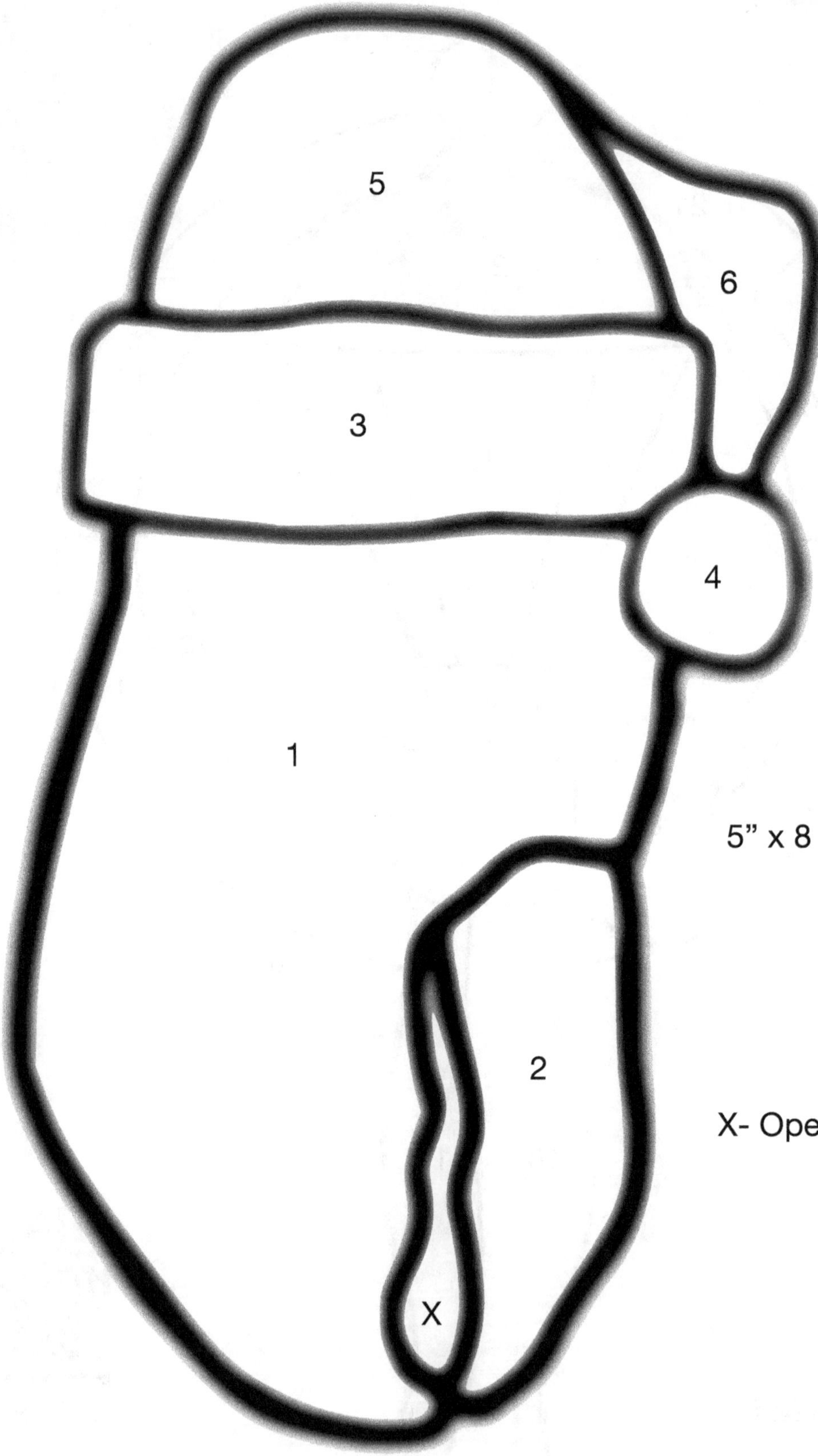

5
6
3
4
1

5" x 8 3/4"

2

X

X- Open Area

Down East Stained Glass

Nouveau Christmas Ornaments

2 sizes

Copper wire hooks and loops can use real hangers

Down East Stained Glass

Christmas Abstract Ornaments

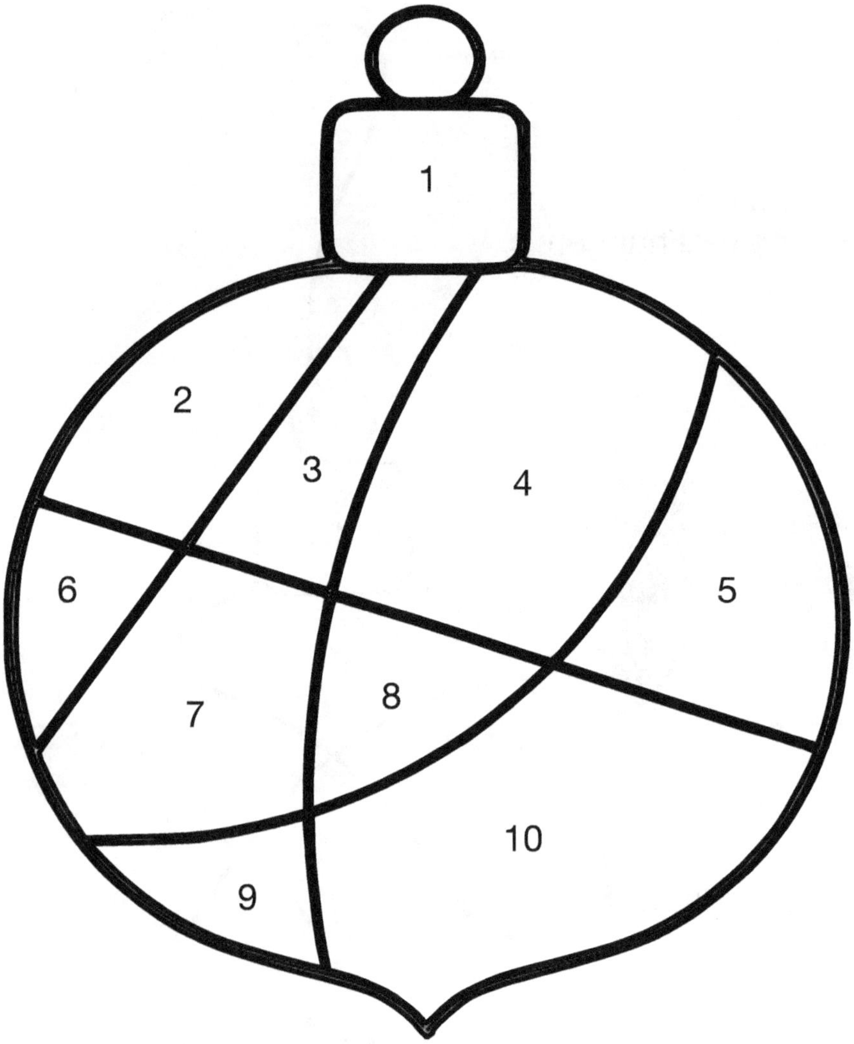

4 1/2" x 5 1/2"

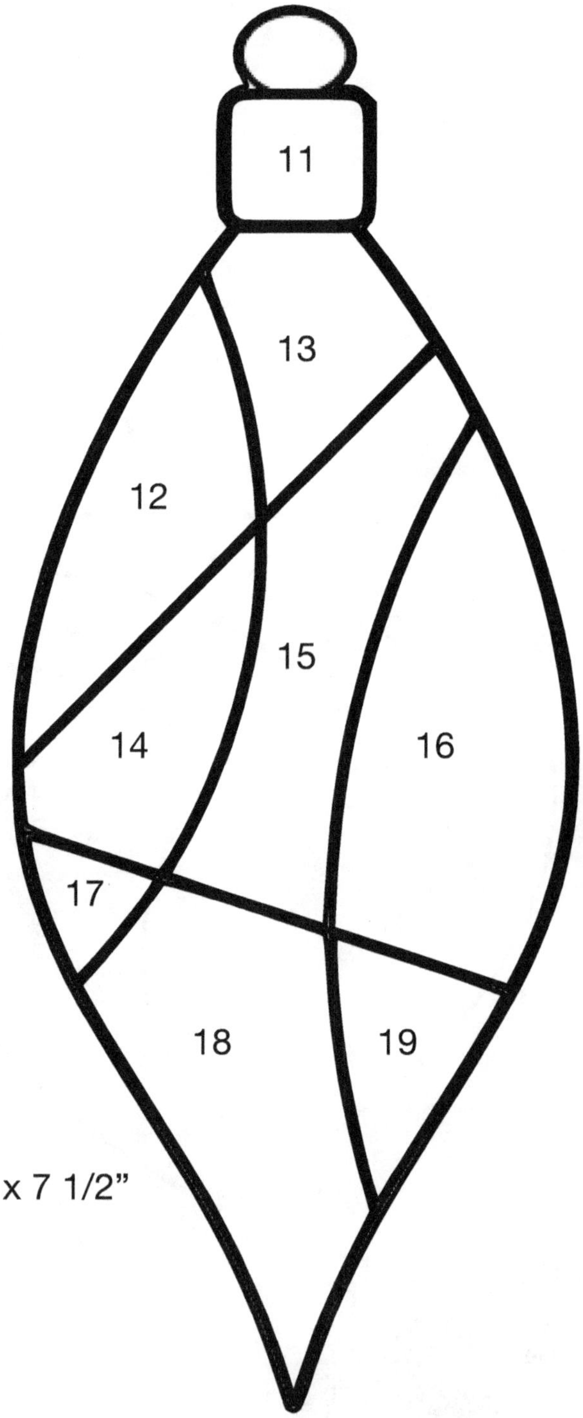

3 1/2" x 7 1/2"

Down East Stained Glass

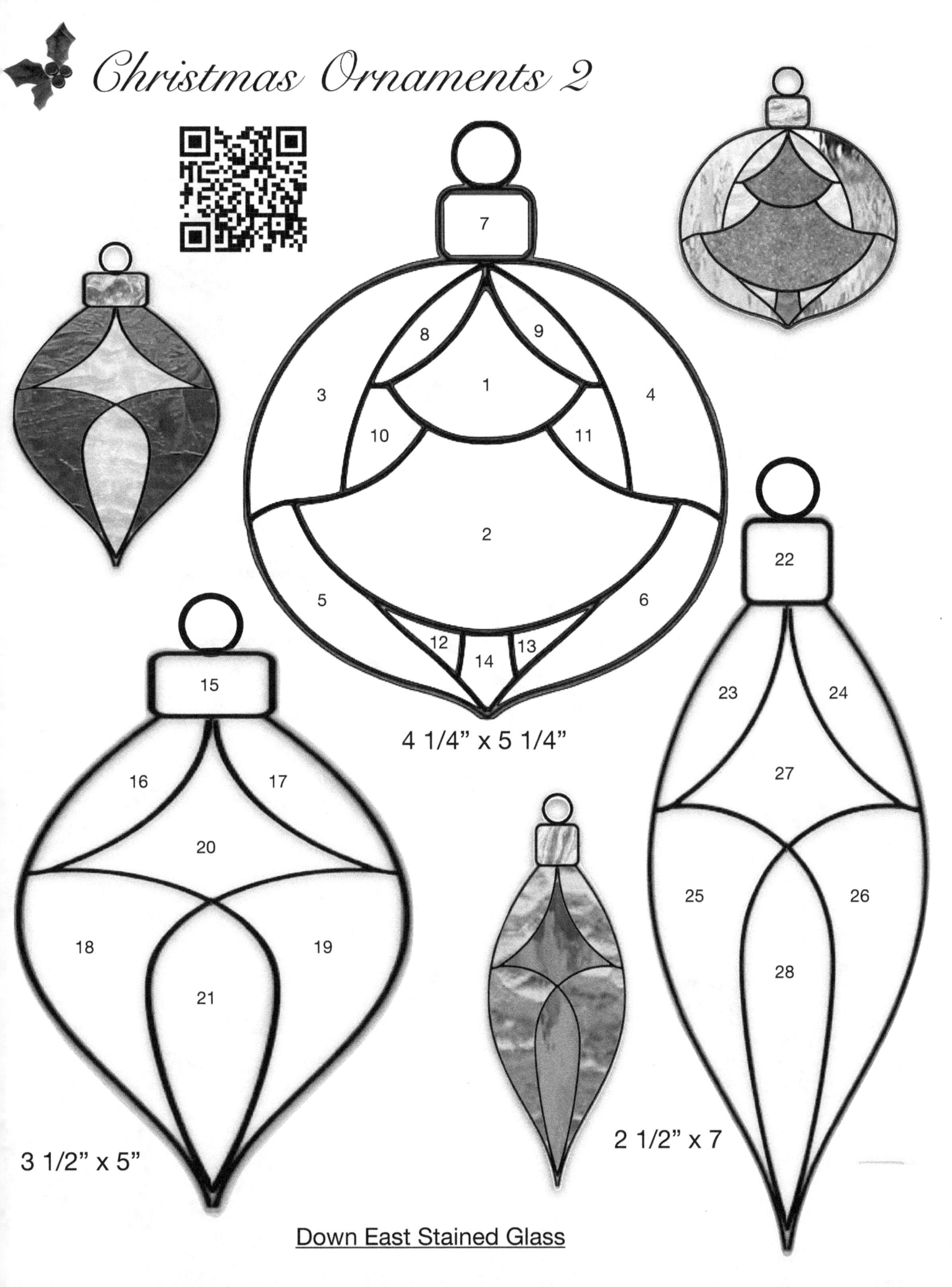

Christmas Ornaments 3

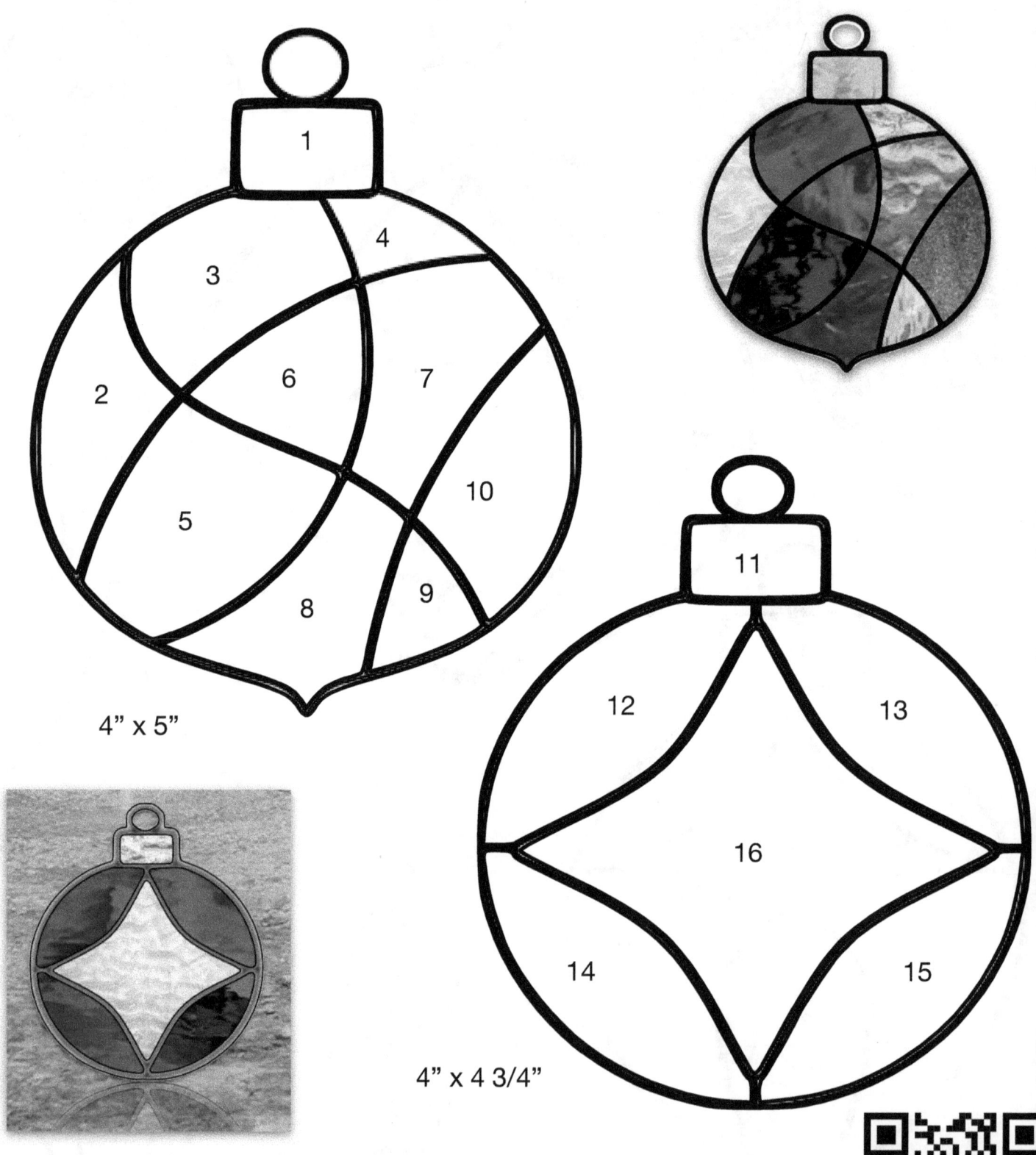

4" x 5"

4" x 4 3/4"

Down East Stained Glass

Christmas Ornaments 4

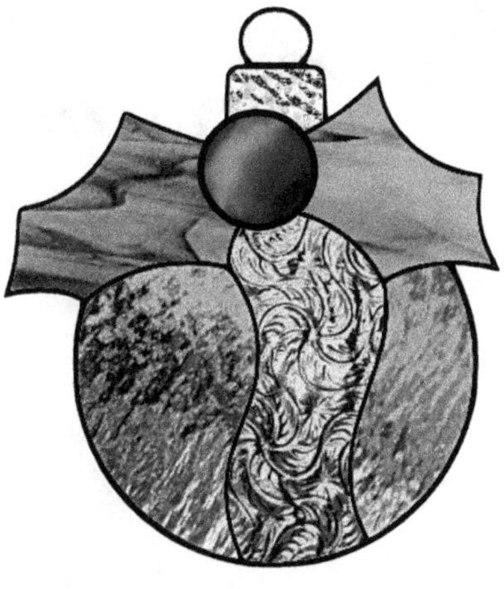

Holly and Bow Patterns

X- May be jewel or glob.

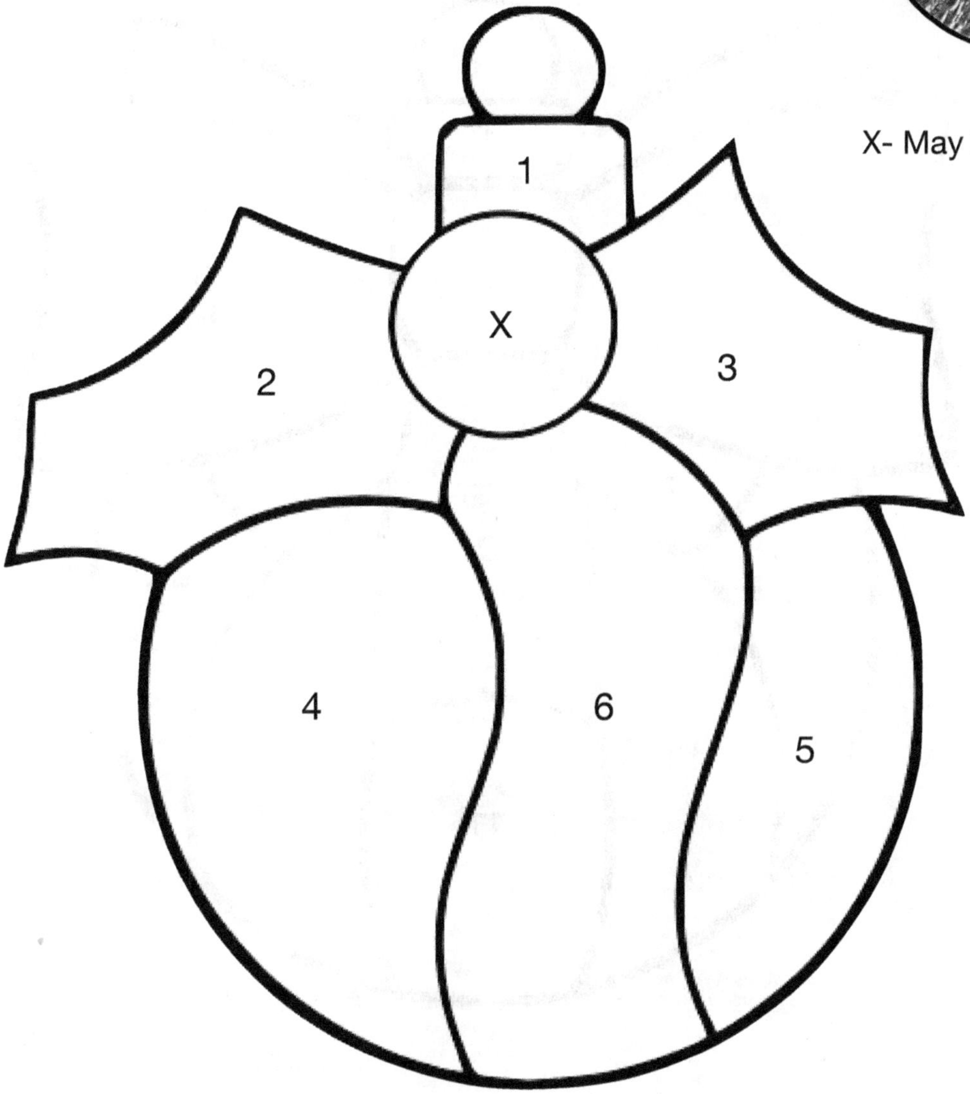

5" x 5"

Down East Stained Glass

Christmas Ornaments 4

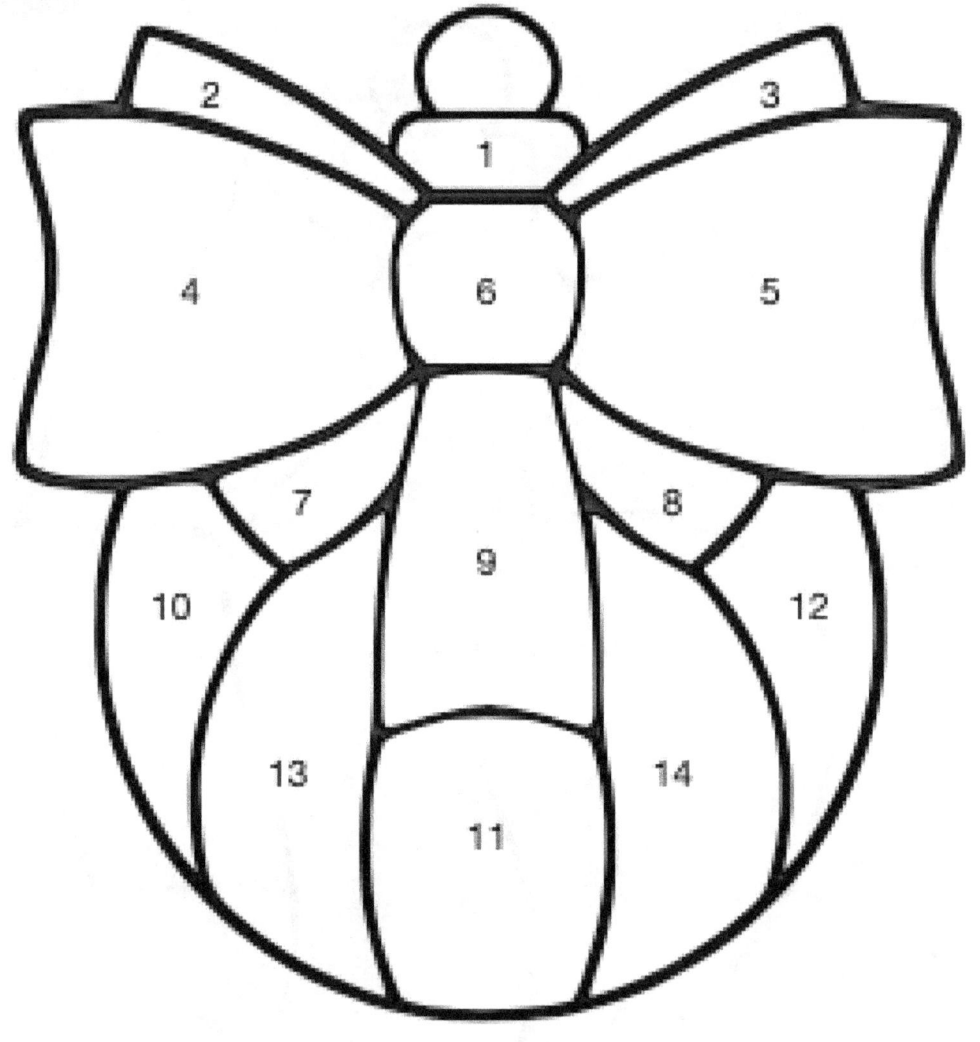

5" x 5"

Down East Stained Glass

Christmas Ornaments

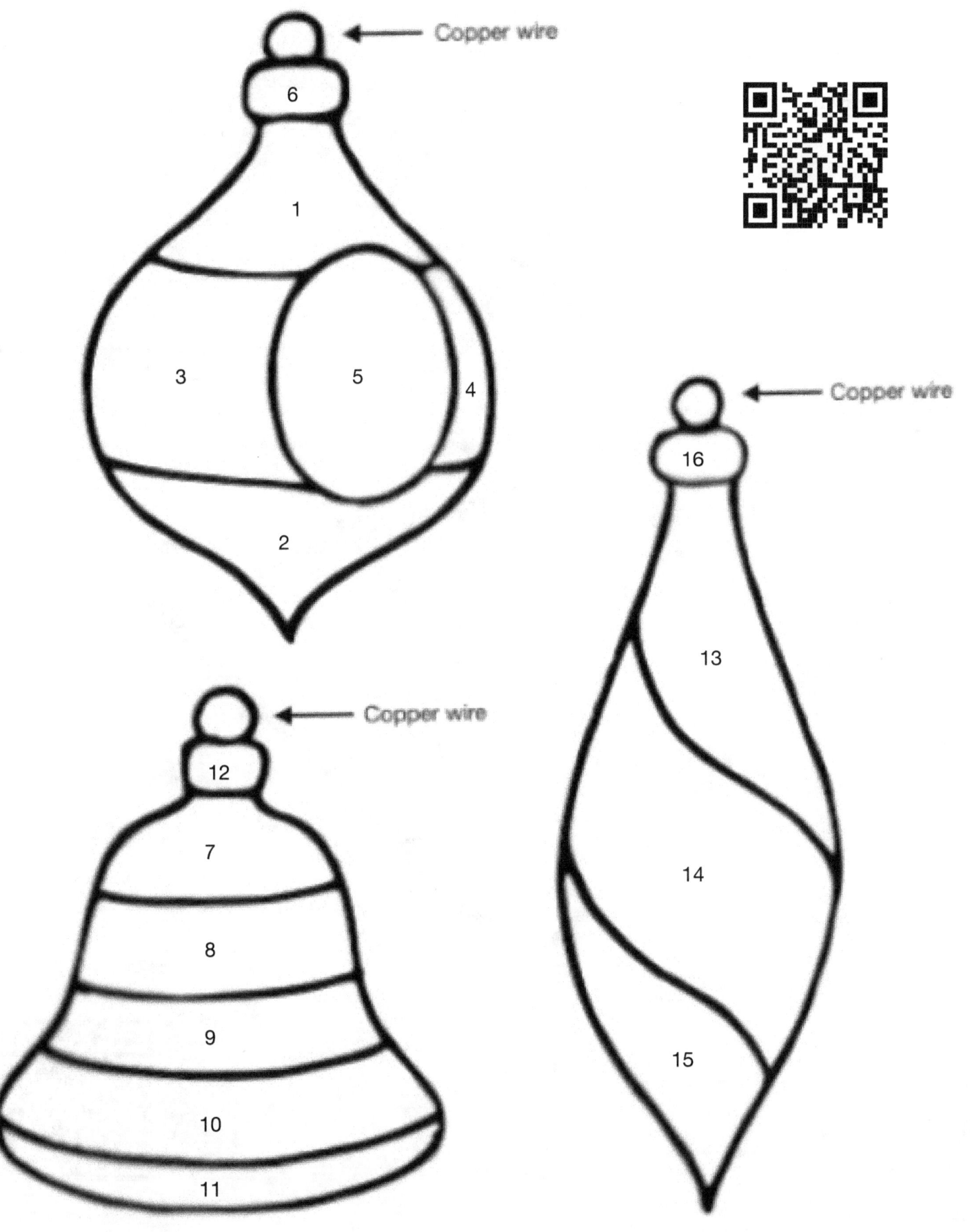

Christmas Tree
Spinner and Hanger

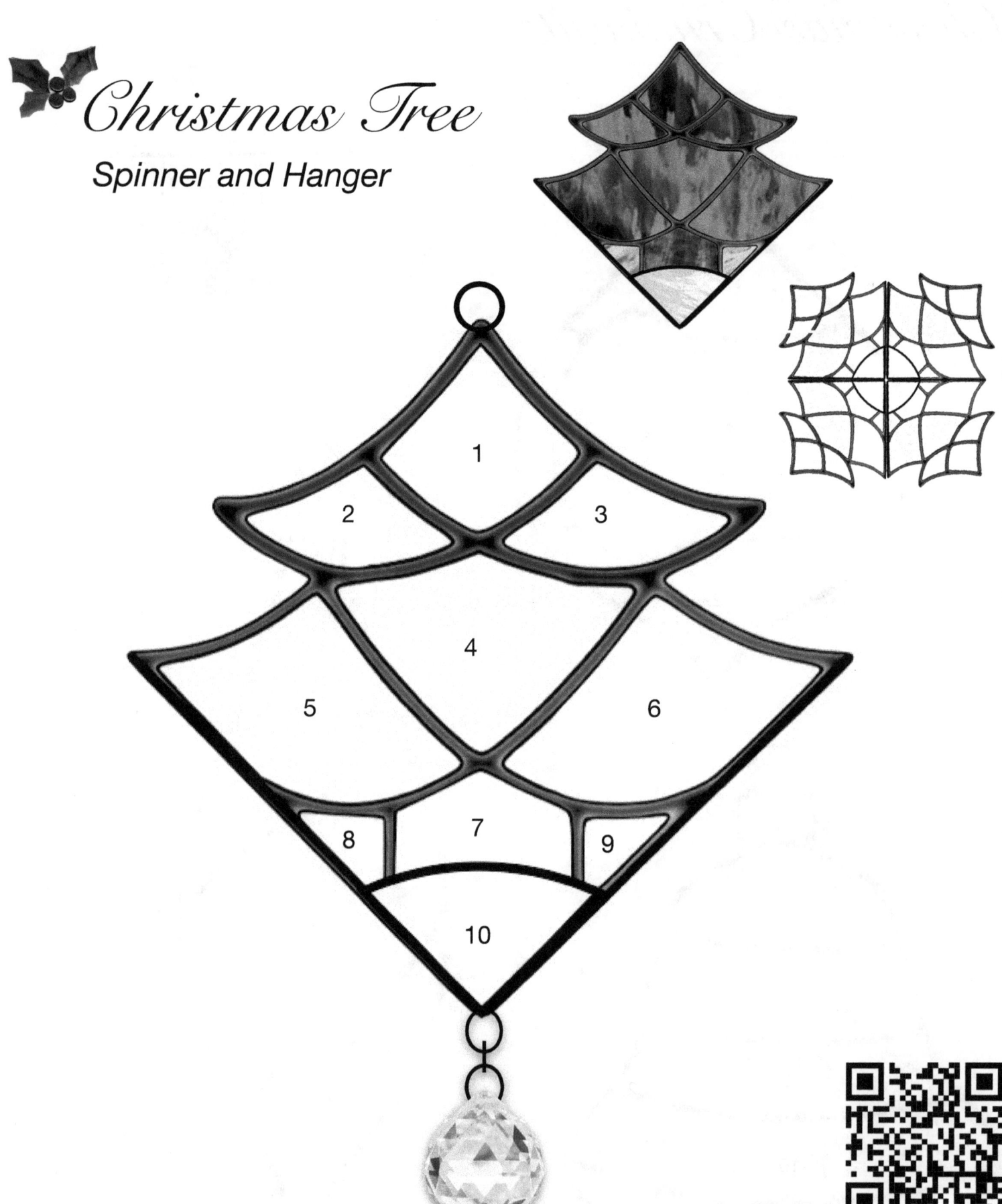

Down East Stained Glass

Christmas Star Ornament
2 size options

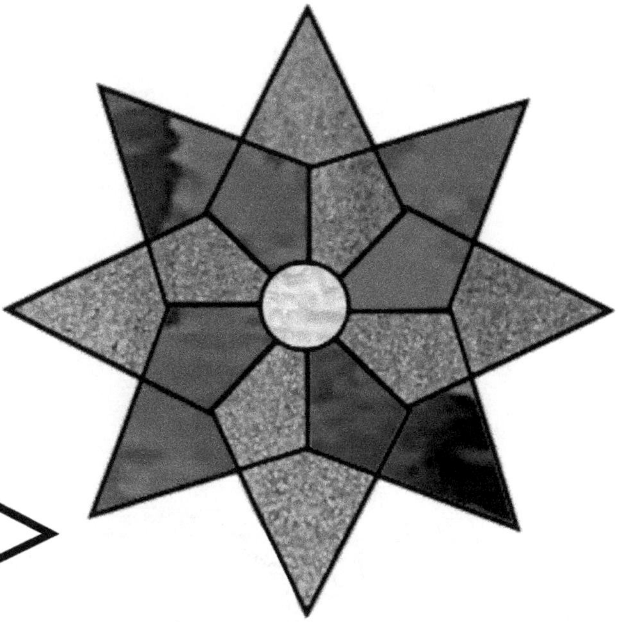

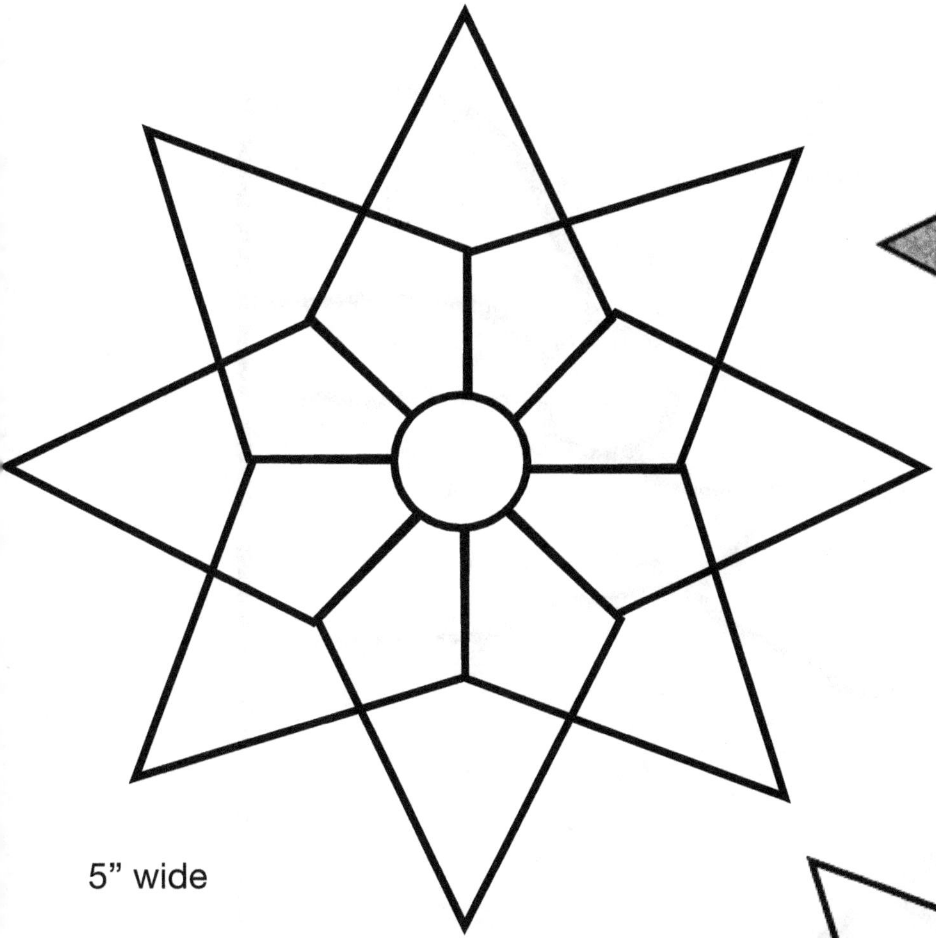

5" wide

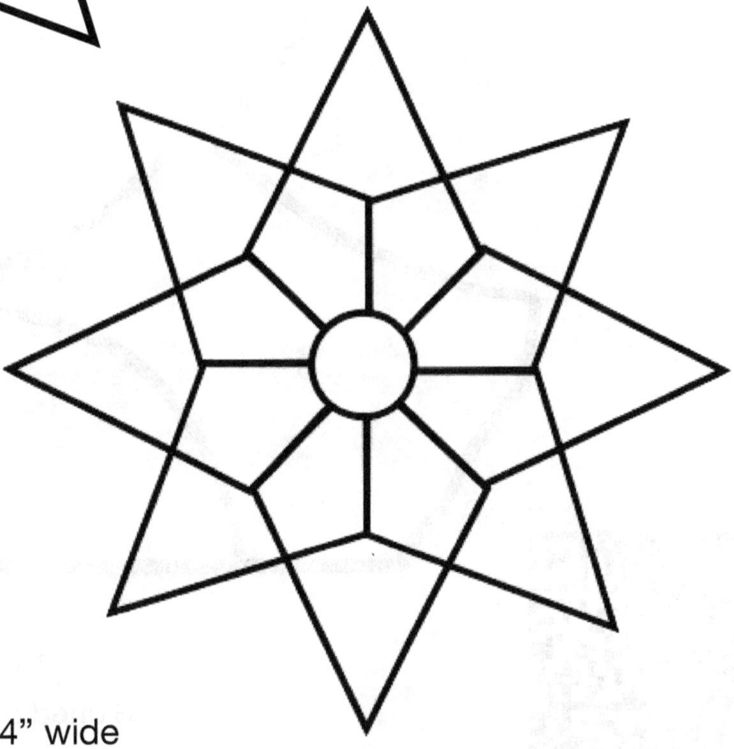

4" wide

Down East Stained Glass

Christmas Tree Bookend
Use with bookend stand

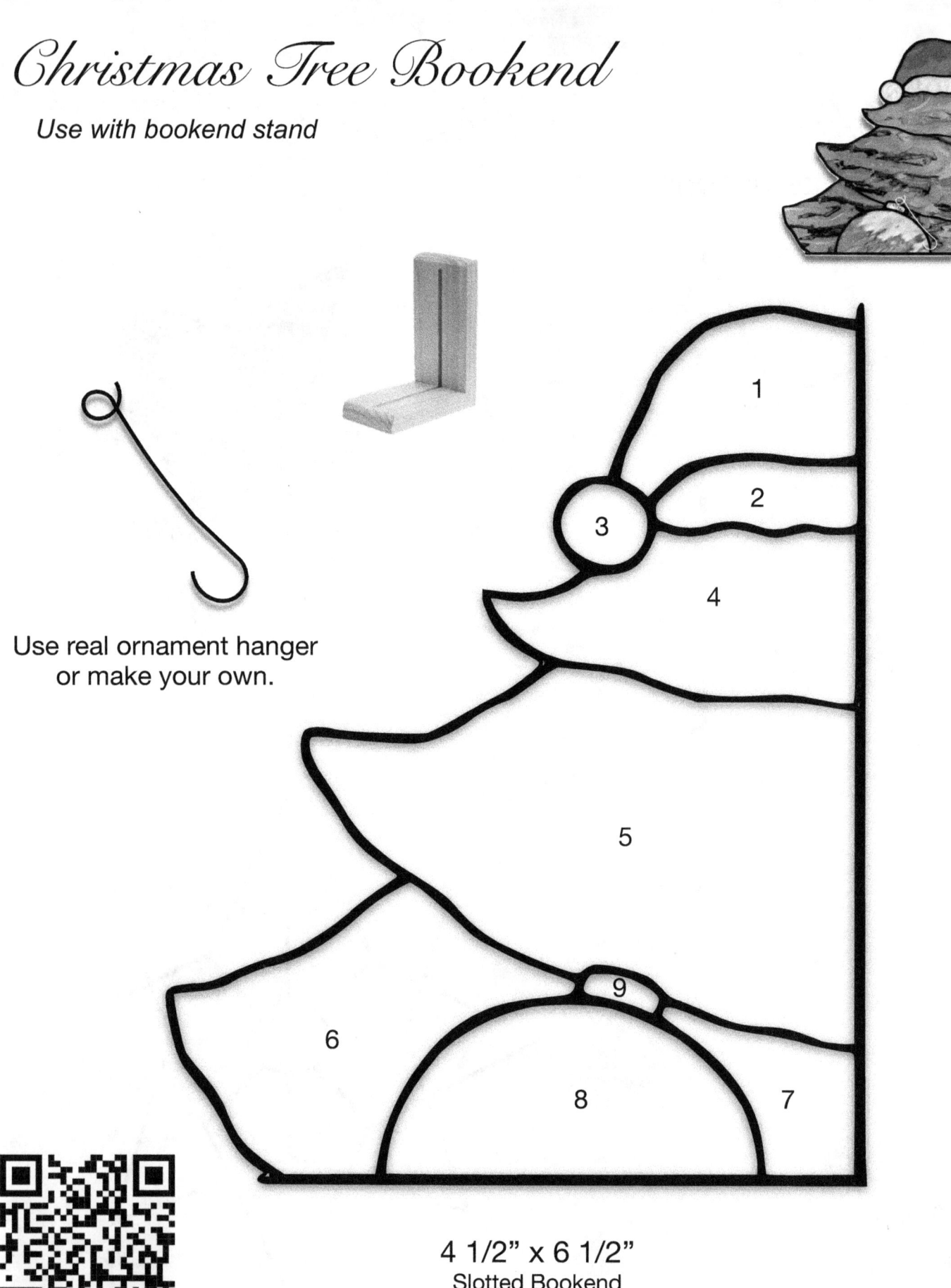

Use real ornament hanger or make your own.

4 1/2" x 6 1/2"
Slotted Bookend

Down East Stained Glass

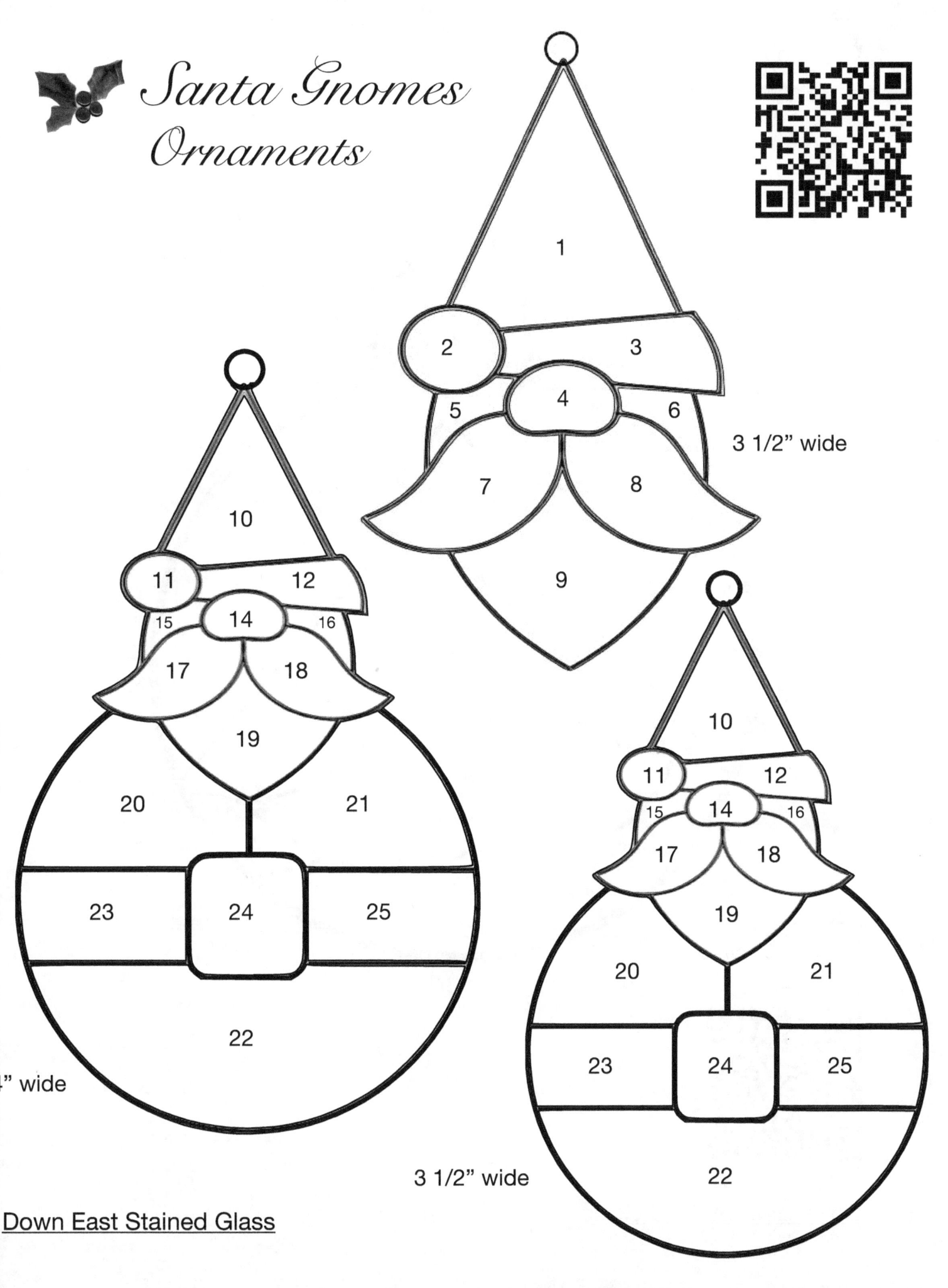

Christmas Tree Star Ornament

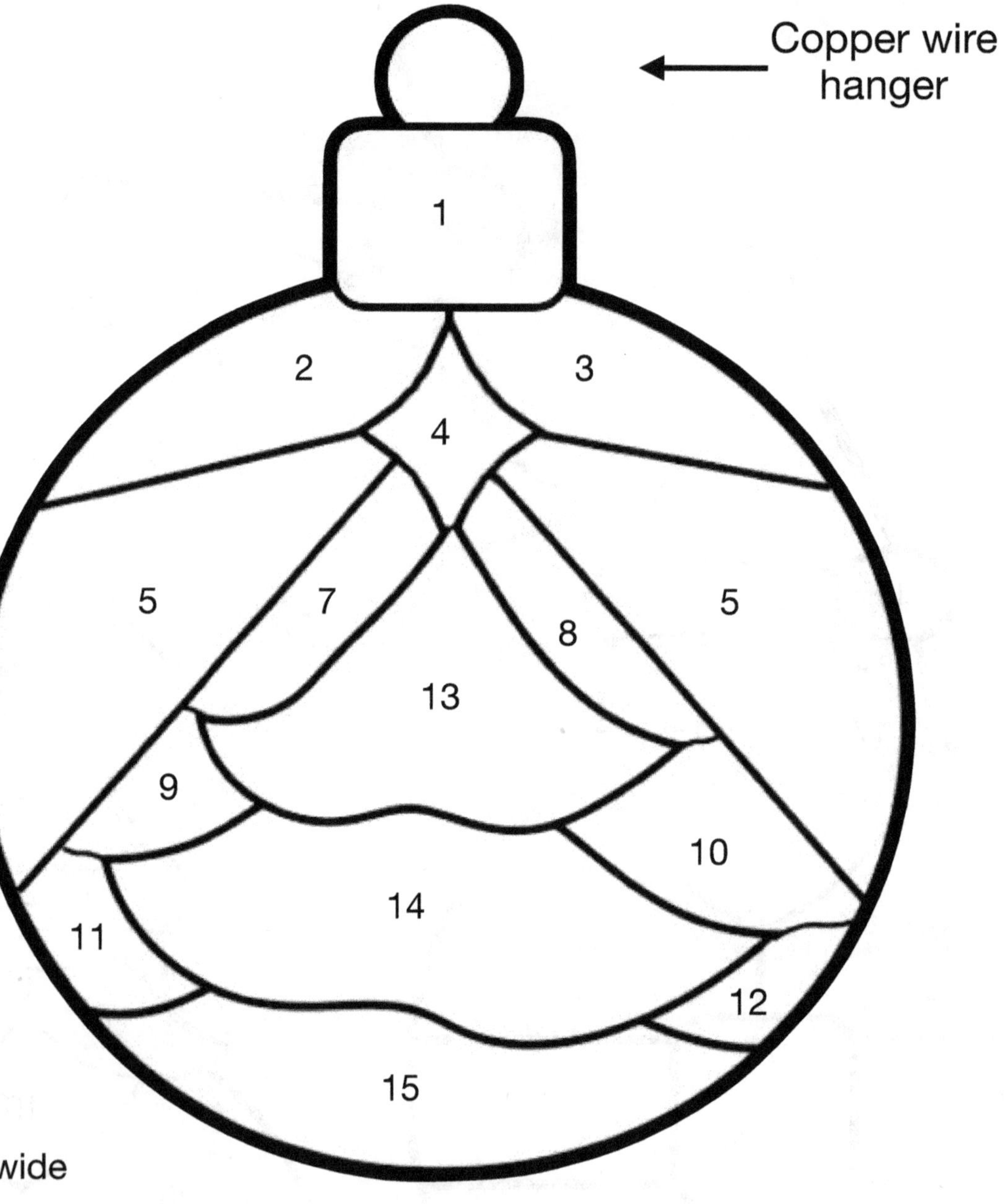

← Copper wire hanger

5" wide

Down East Stained Glass

Christmas Tree Teardrop

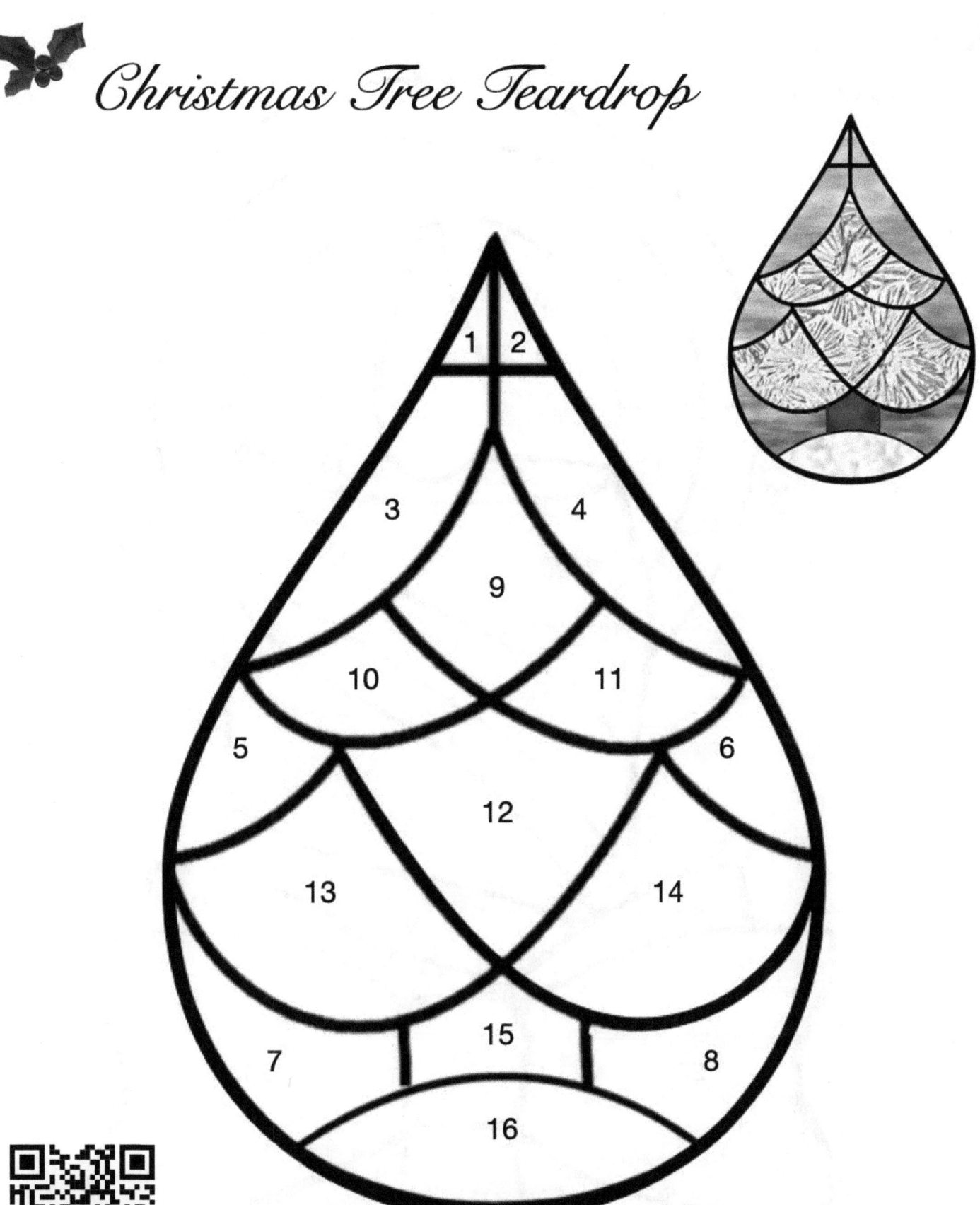

5" x 7 1/2"

Down East Stained Glass

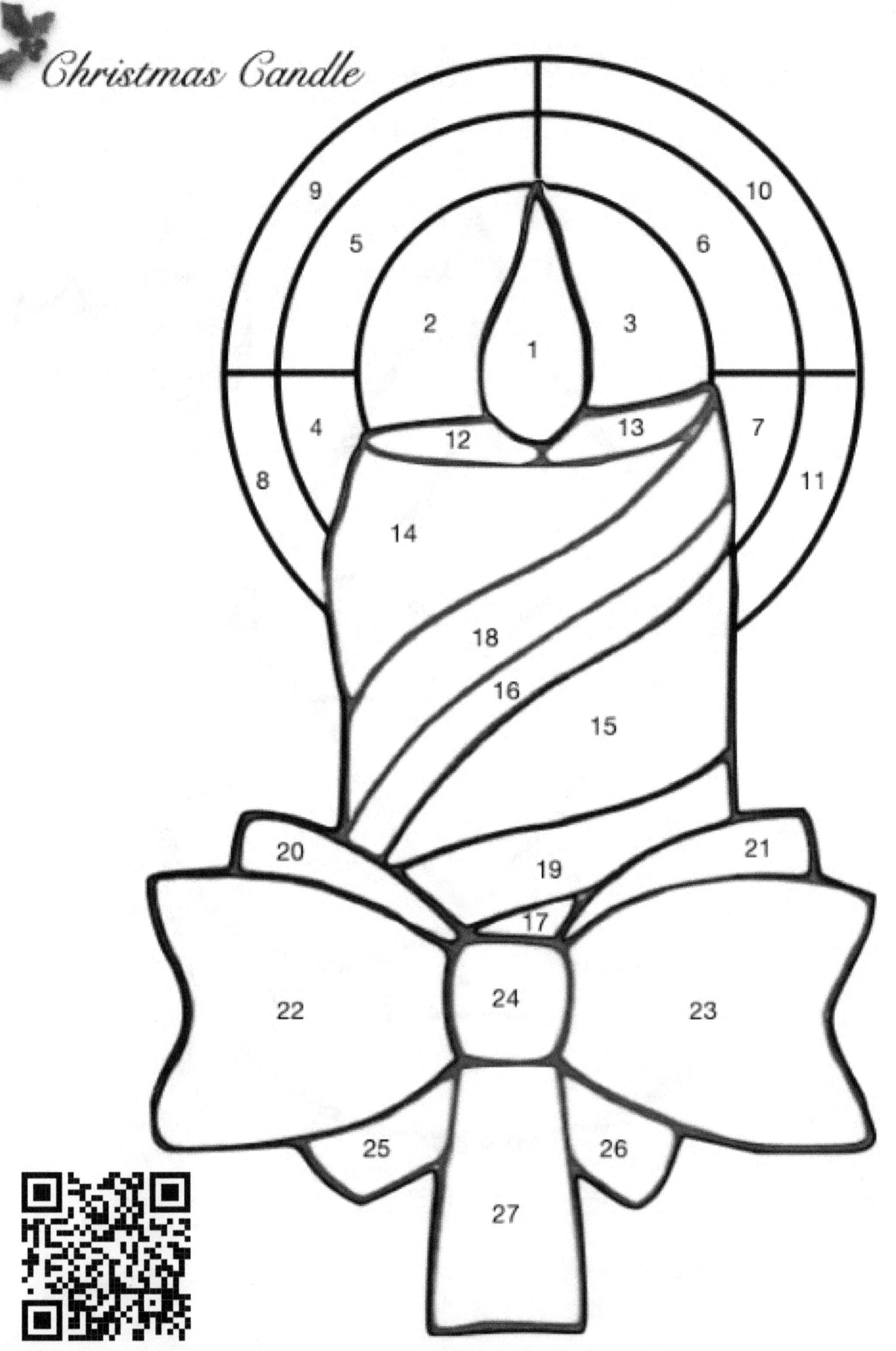

Deco 2 Christmas Ornament

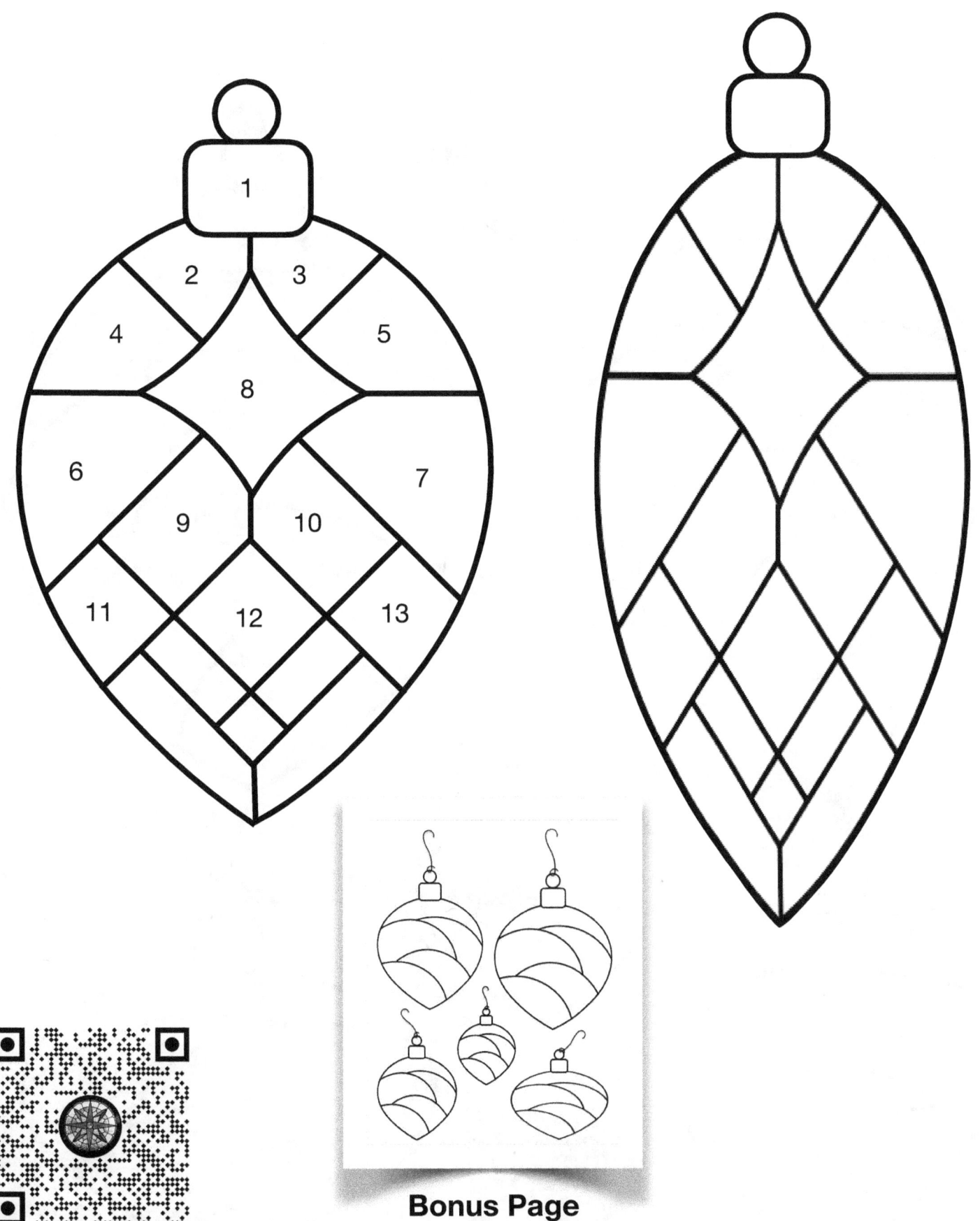

Bonus Page

Down East Stained Glass

Bonus Page

Christmas Daisy Ornament

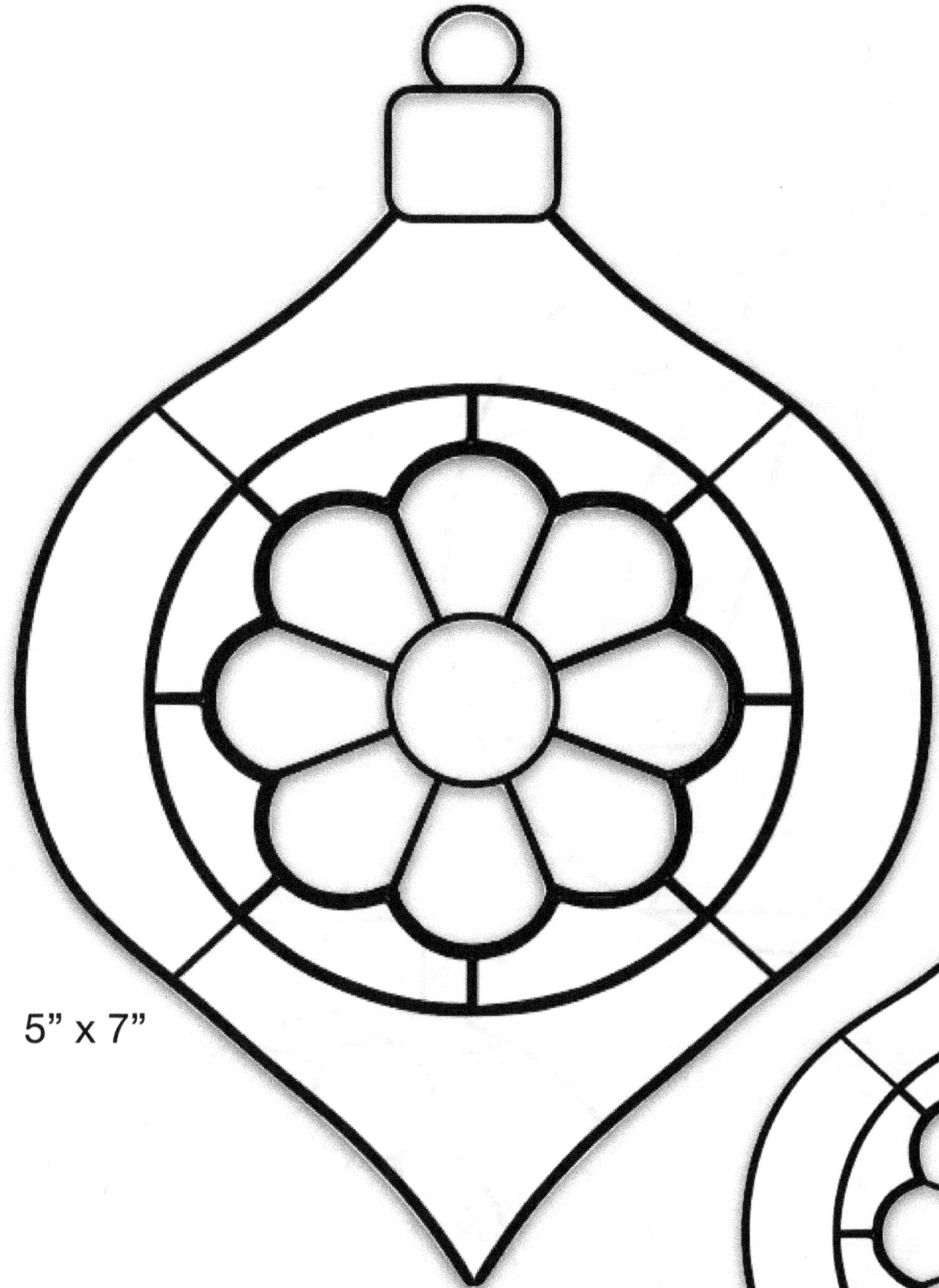

5" x 7"

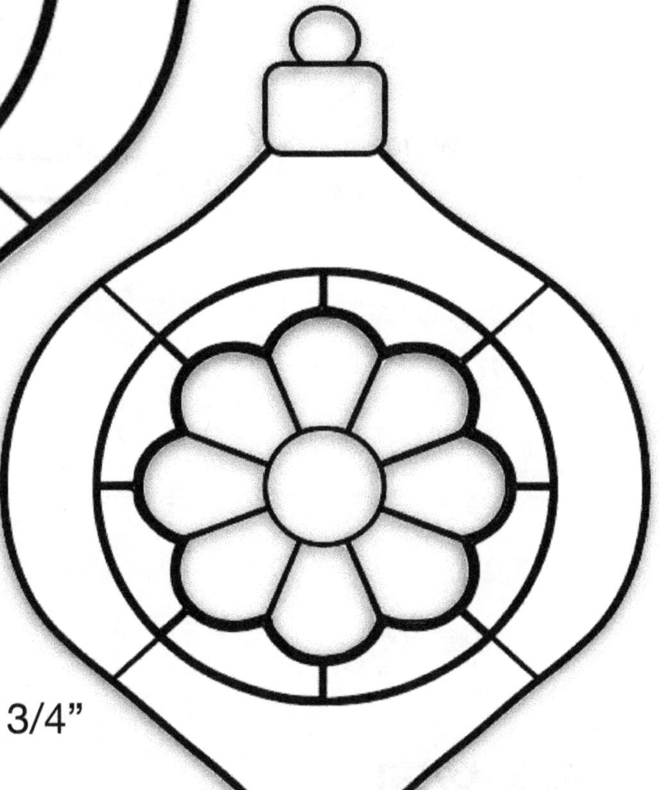

3 1/2" x 4 3/4"

Down East Stained Glass

Angel Ornament

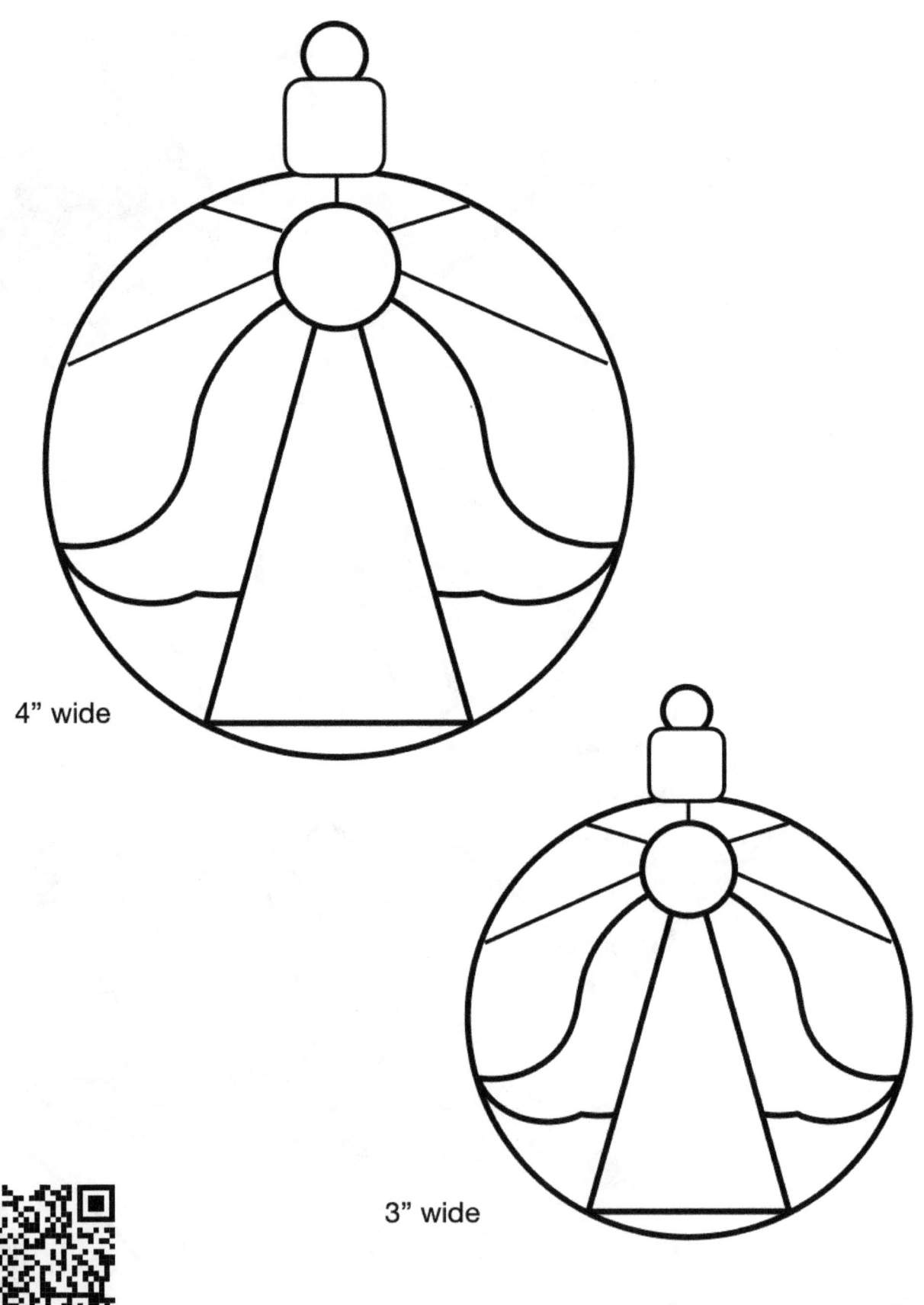

4" wide

3" wide

Christmas Tree Ornament
3" x 6" and 3"x 4.5"

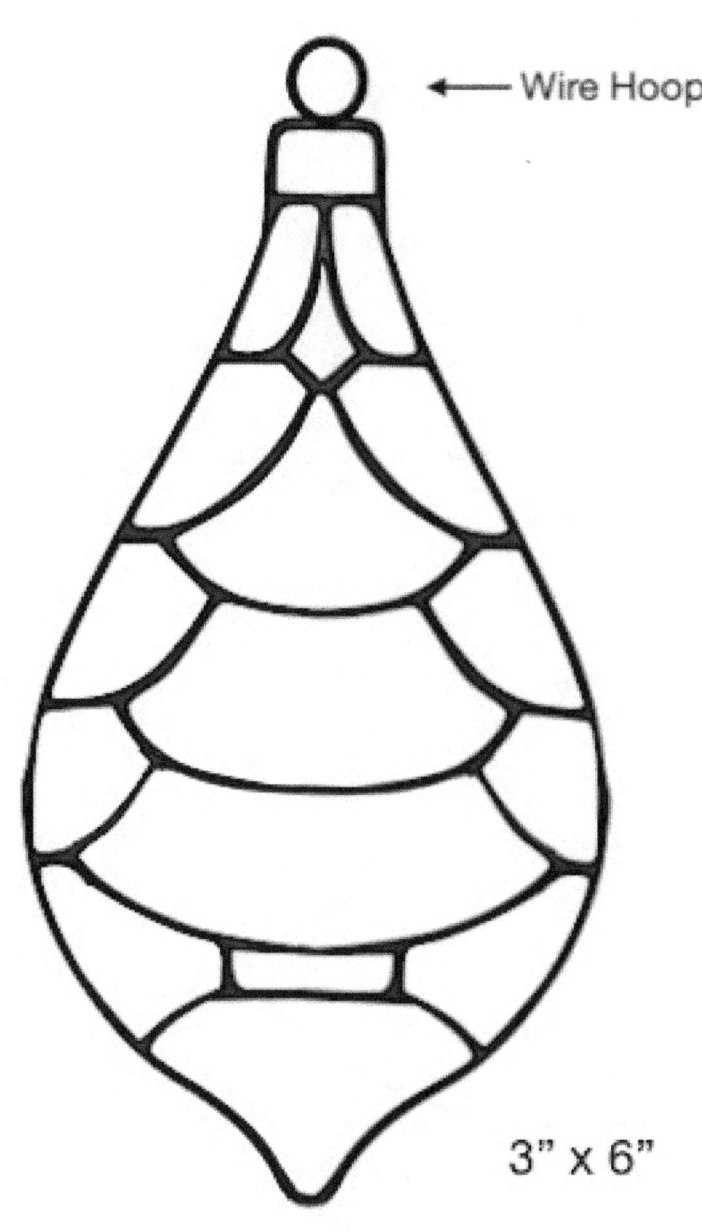

← Wire Hoop

3" x 6"

3" x 4.5"

Easy Christmas Tree

2 sizes

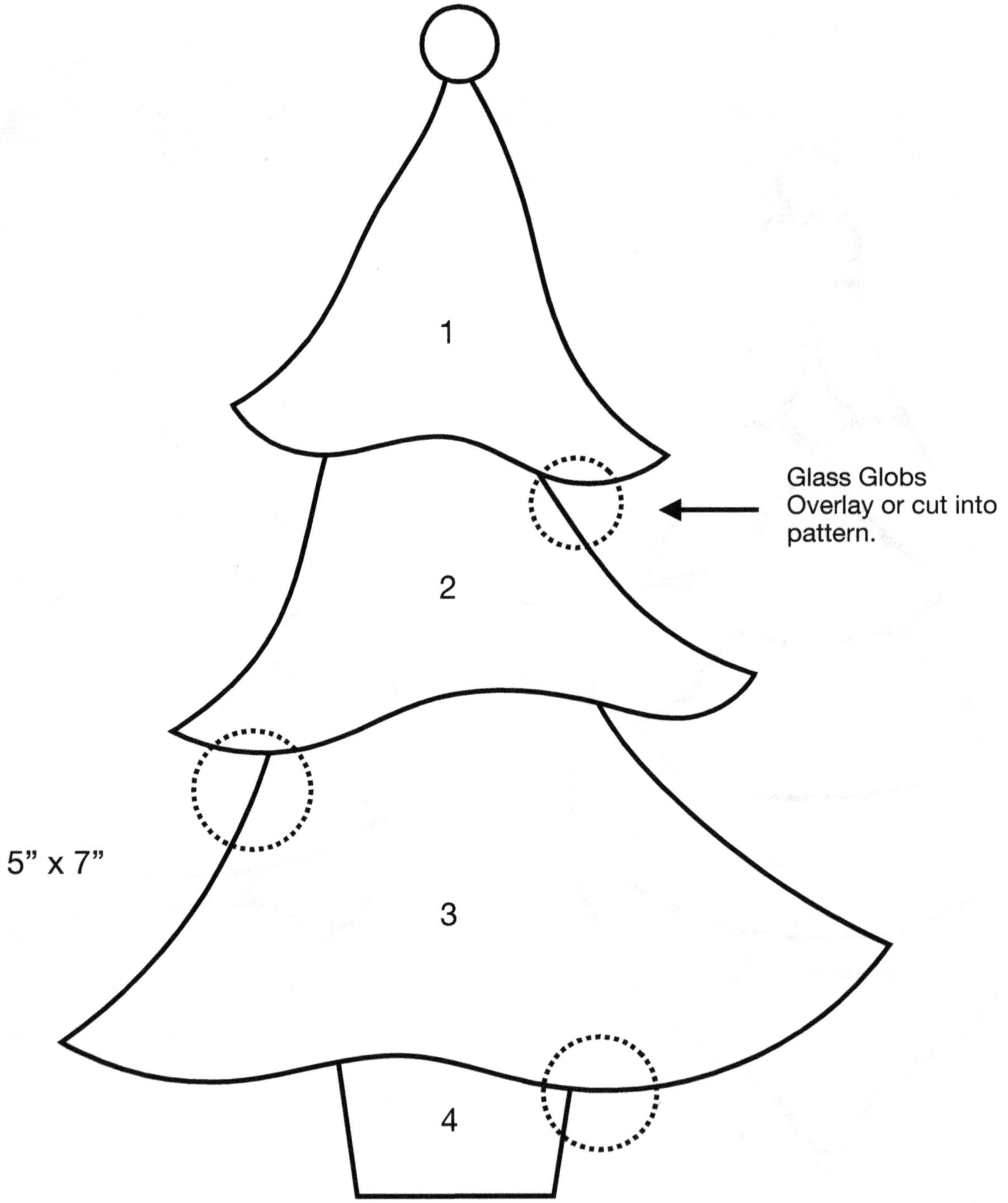

Glass Globs Overlay or cut into pattern.

5" x 7"

Down East Stained Glass

Snowman & Christmas Tree

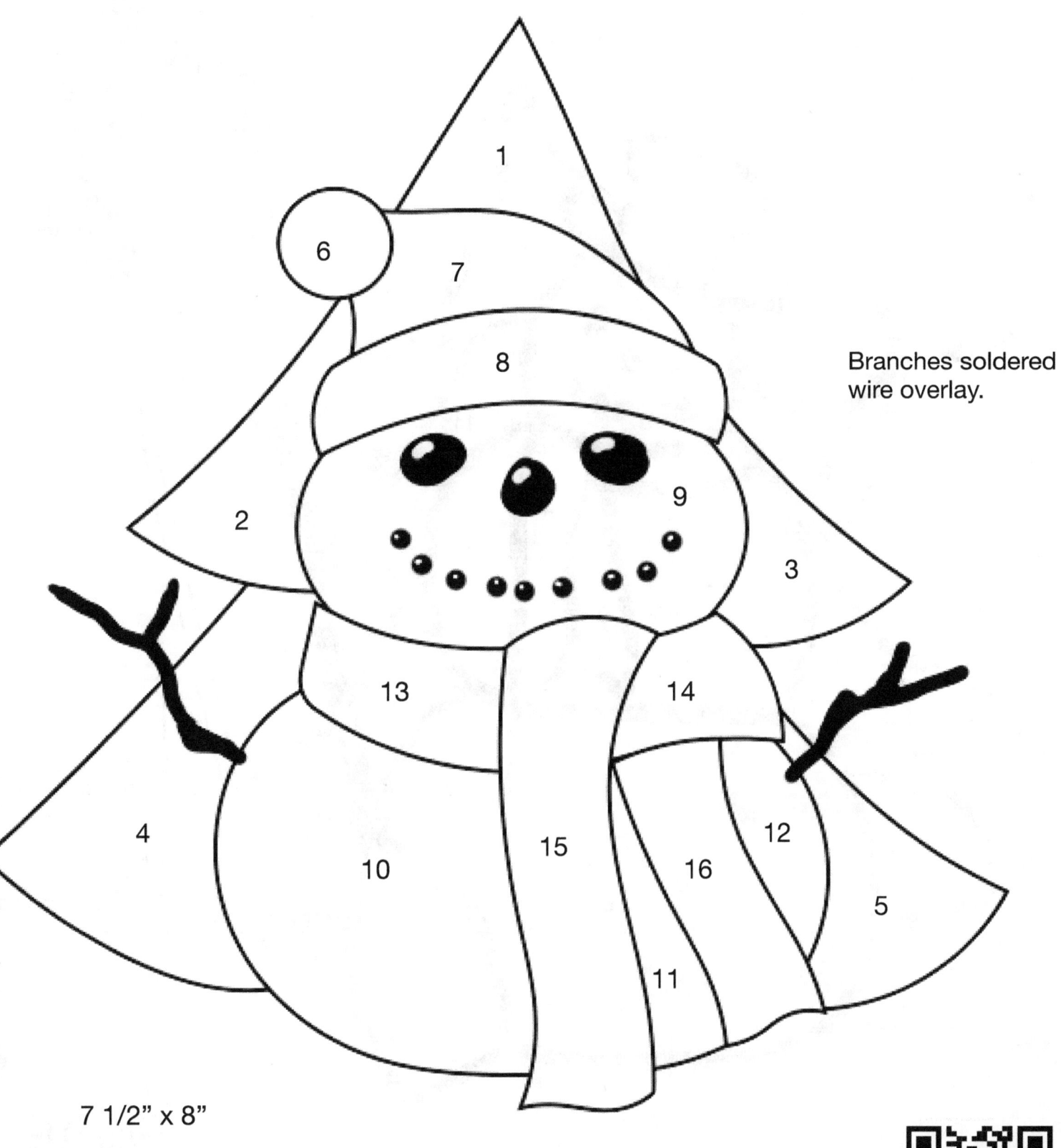

Branches soldered wire overlay.

7 1/2" x 8"

Down East Stained Glass

Snowman

6" x 7 1/2"

Bend wire for broom stick and branches. Hat brim may be one wire. Solder aside and overlay.
Face detail can be painted.

Down East Stained Glass

Snowflake

7 1/2" x 8"

Down East Stained Glass

Luna Moth Snowflake

8 1/4" x 7 1/4"

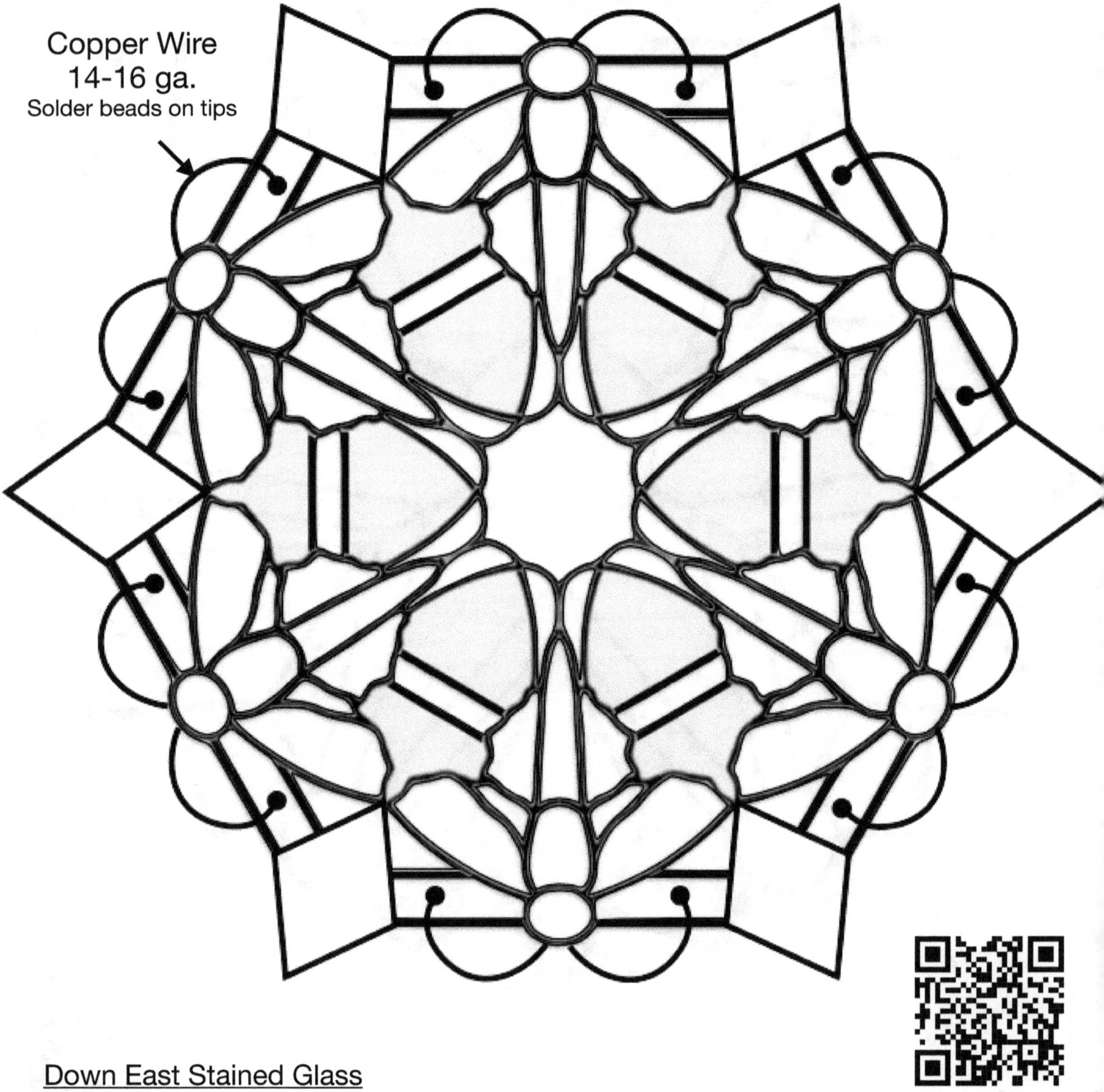

Copper Wire 14-16 ga.
Solder beads on tips

Down East Stained Glass

Snowflake Version #2

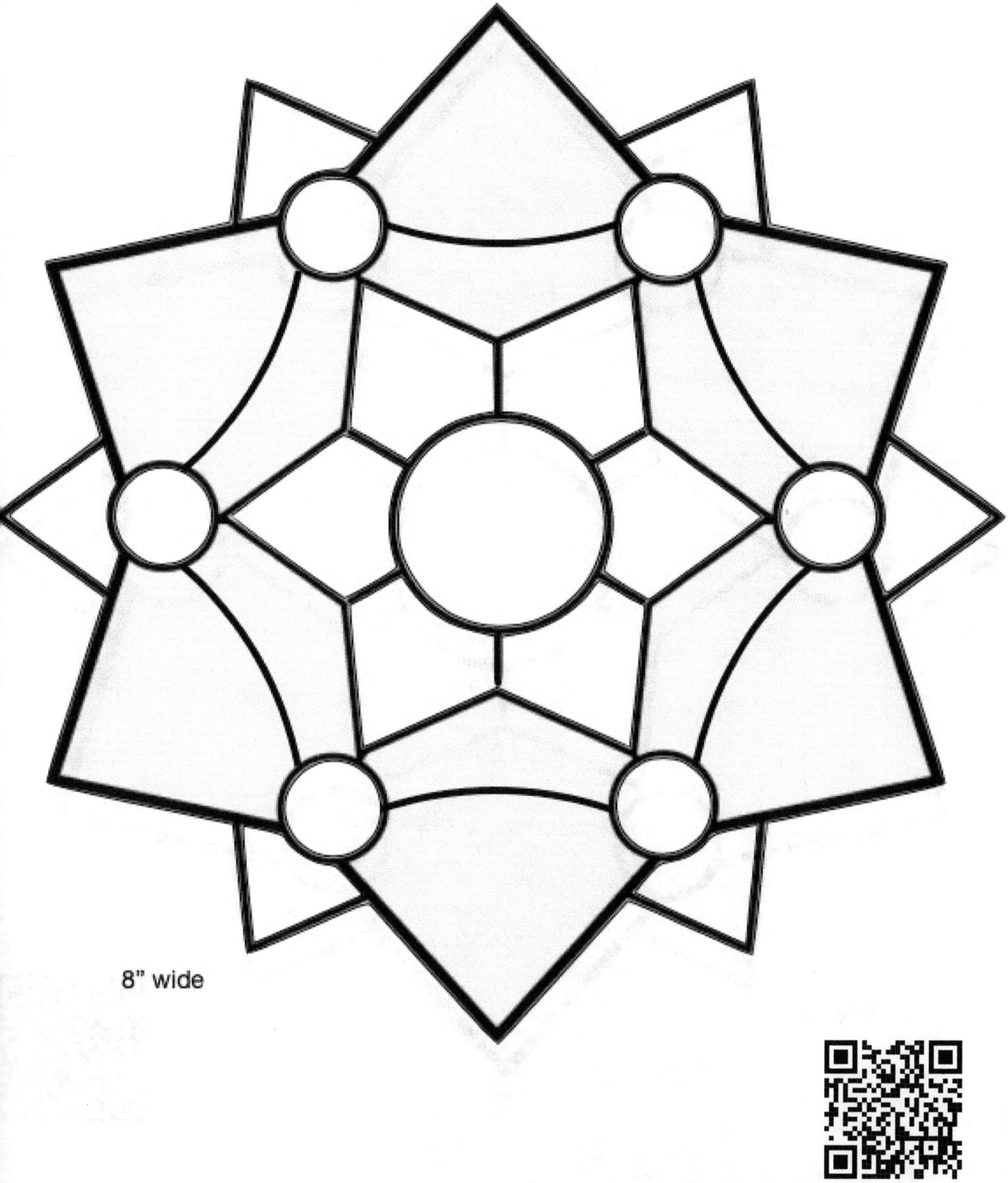

8" wide

Snowflake

Version #3

No numbers optiion

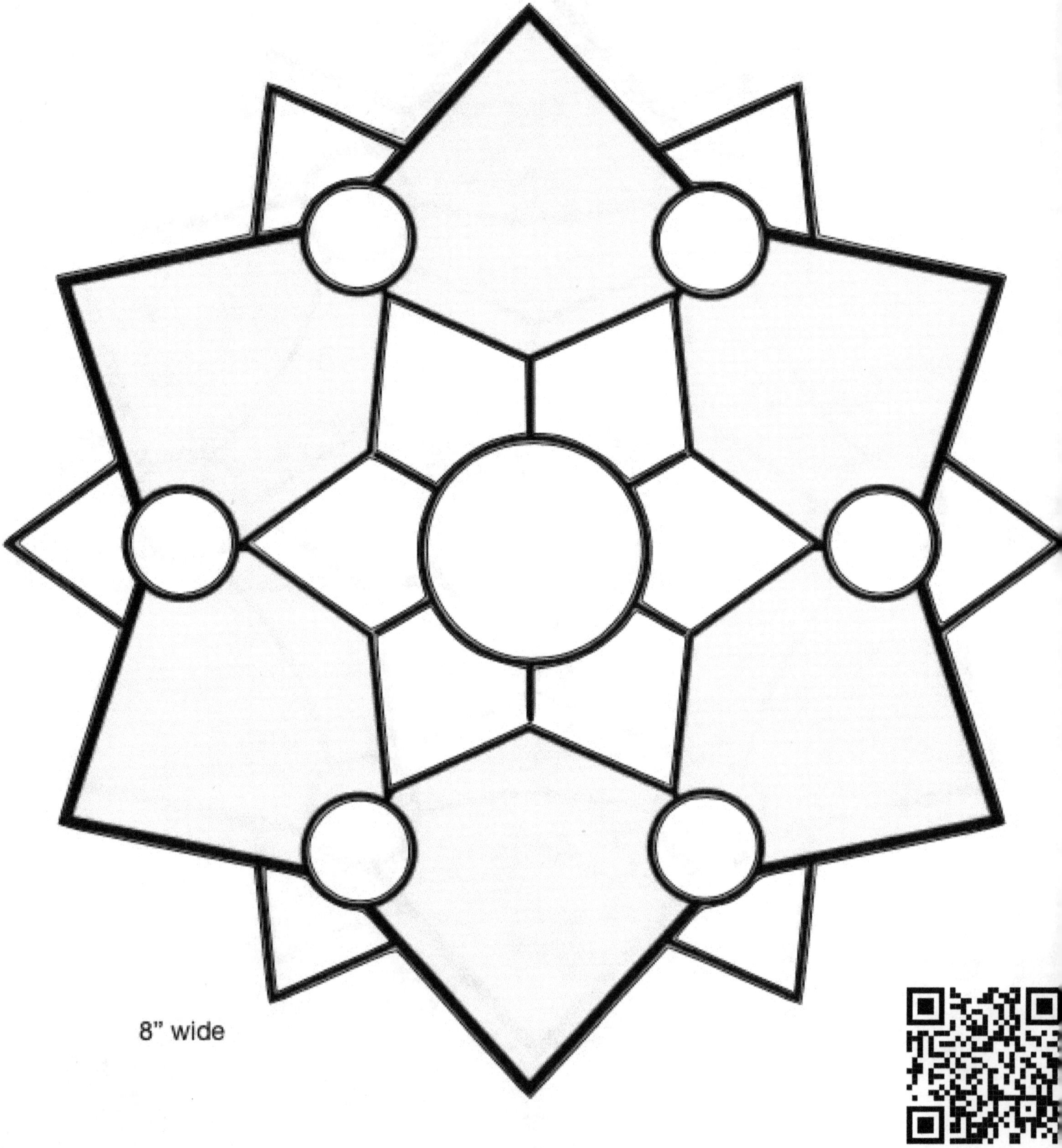

8" wide

Gnome Snowflake

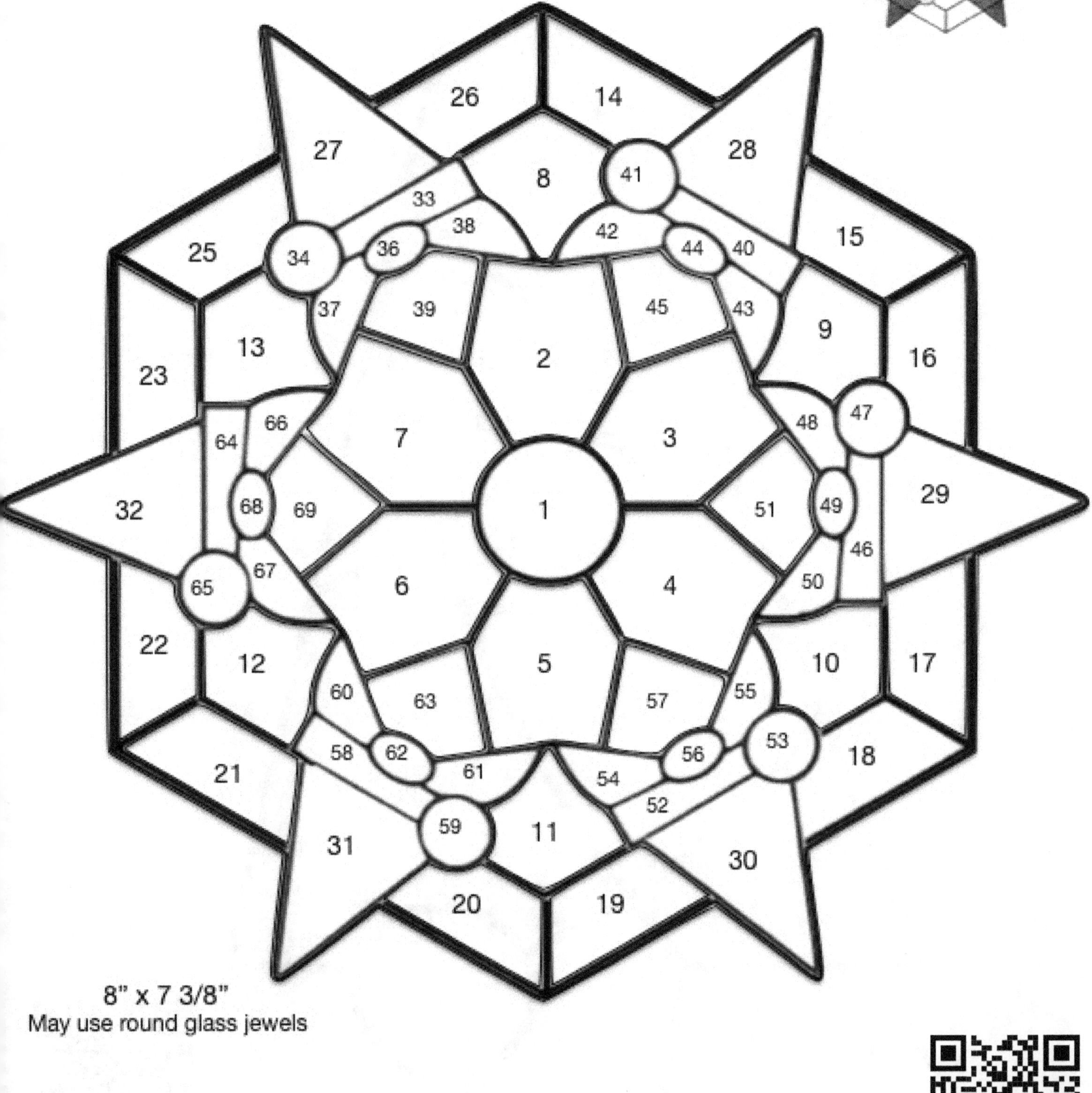

8" x 7 3/8"
May use round glass jewels

Down East Stained Glass

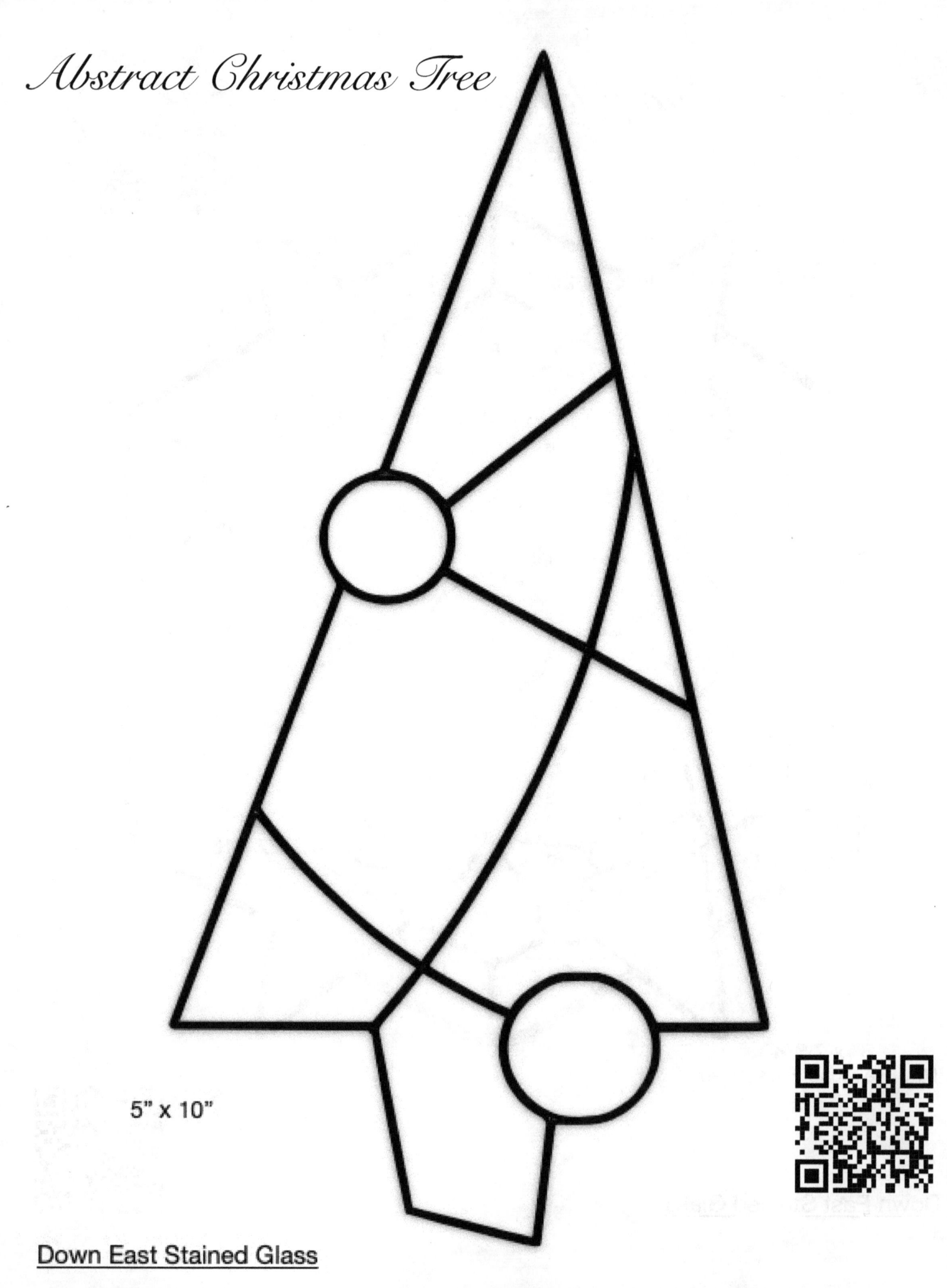

Mistletoe Hanger
7 1/2" wide

X - Open areas no glass.

Down East Stained Glass

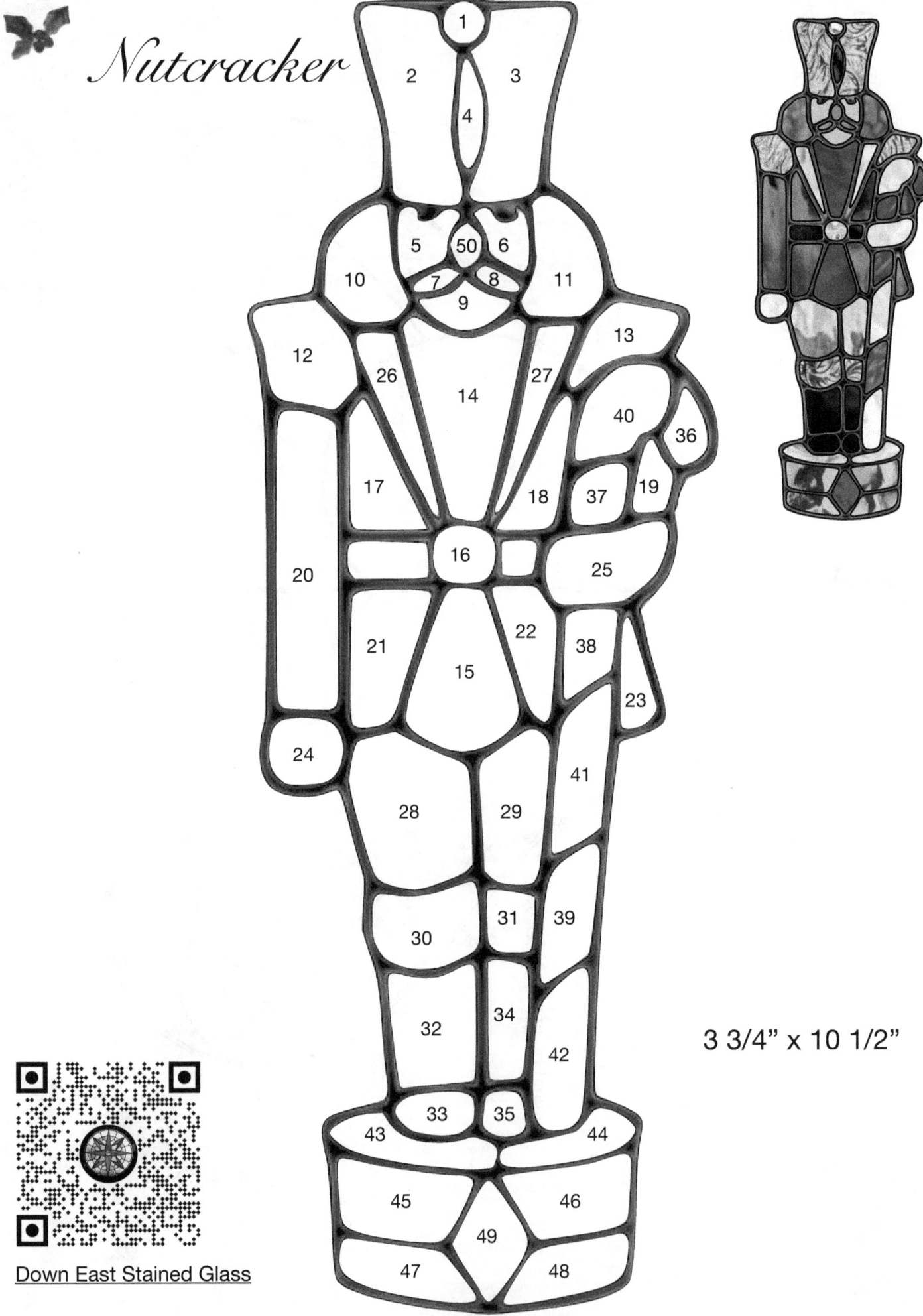

Nutcracker Face

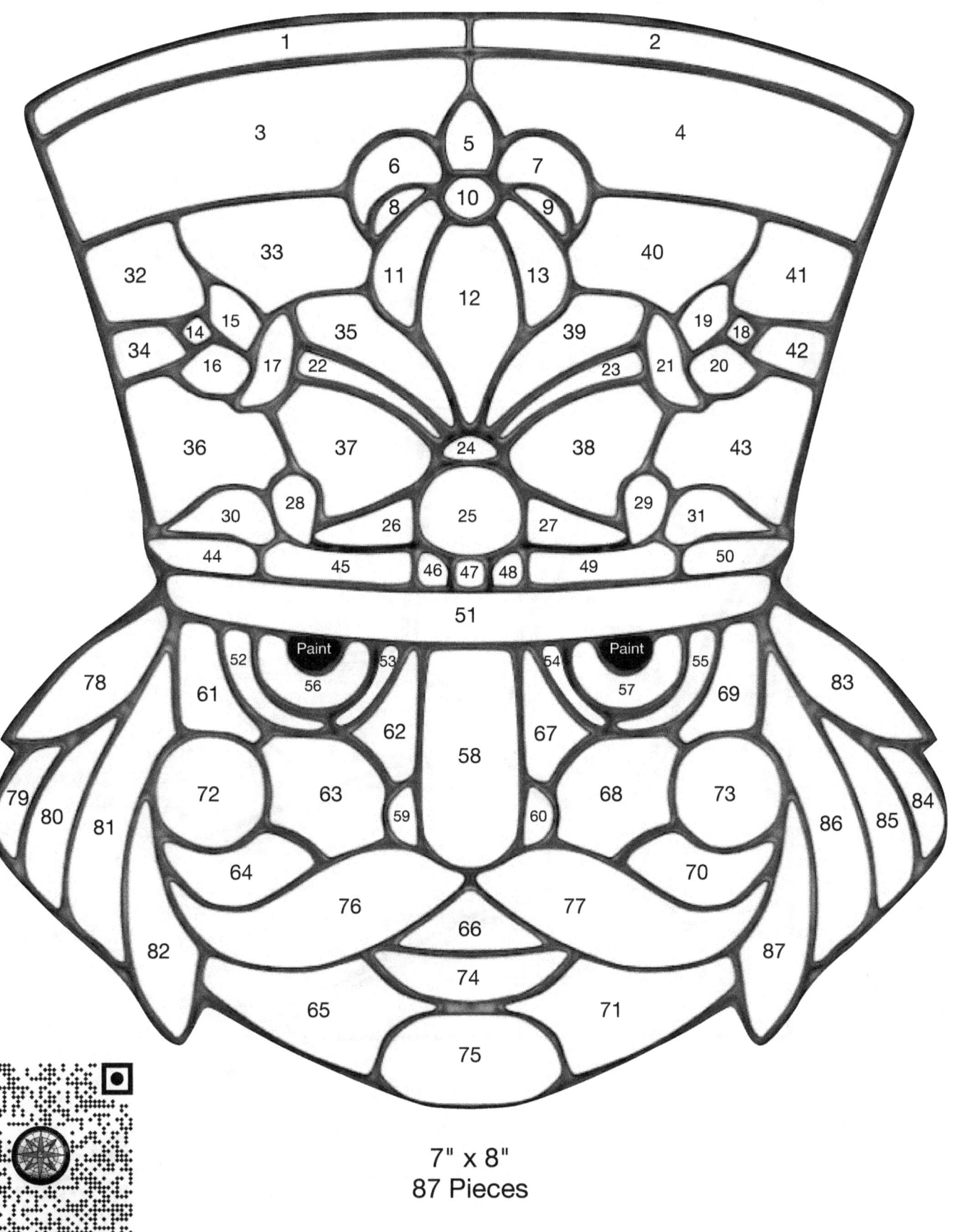

7" x 8"
87 Pieces

Down East Stained Glass

Snowflake Spinner

8" spinner 6 of each pattern

4 Options

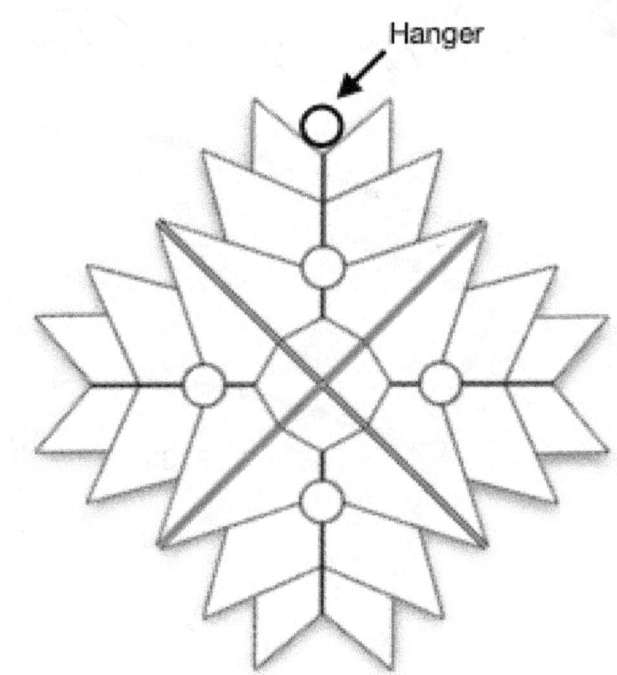

Hanger

Version #1
4" x 4"

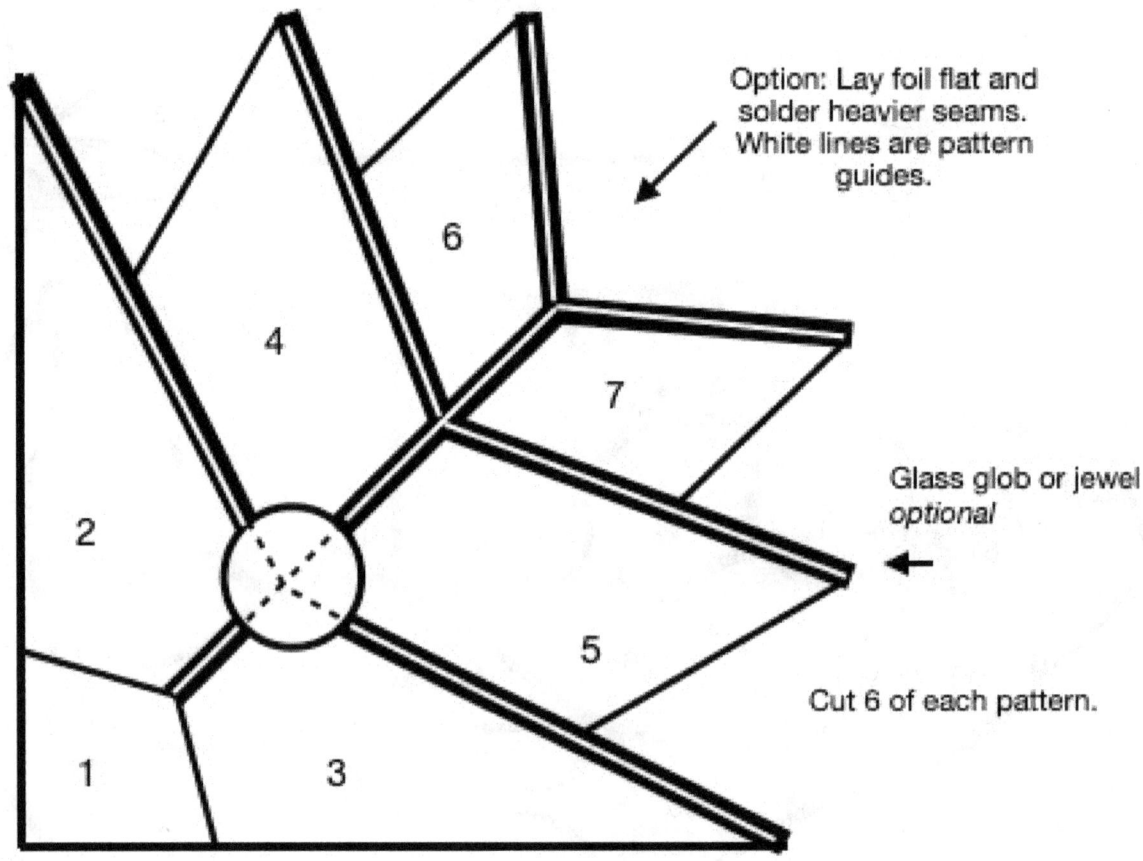

Option: Lay foil flat and solder heavier seams. White lines are pattern guides.

Glass glob or jewel *optional*

Cut 6 of each pattern.

Down East Stained Glass

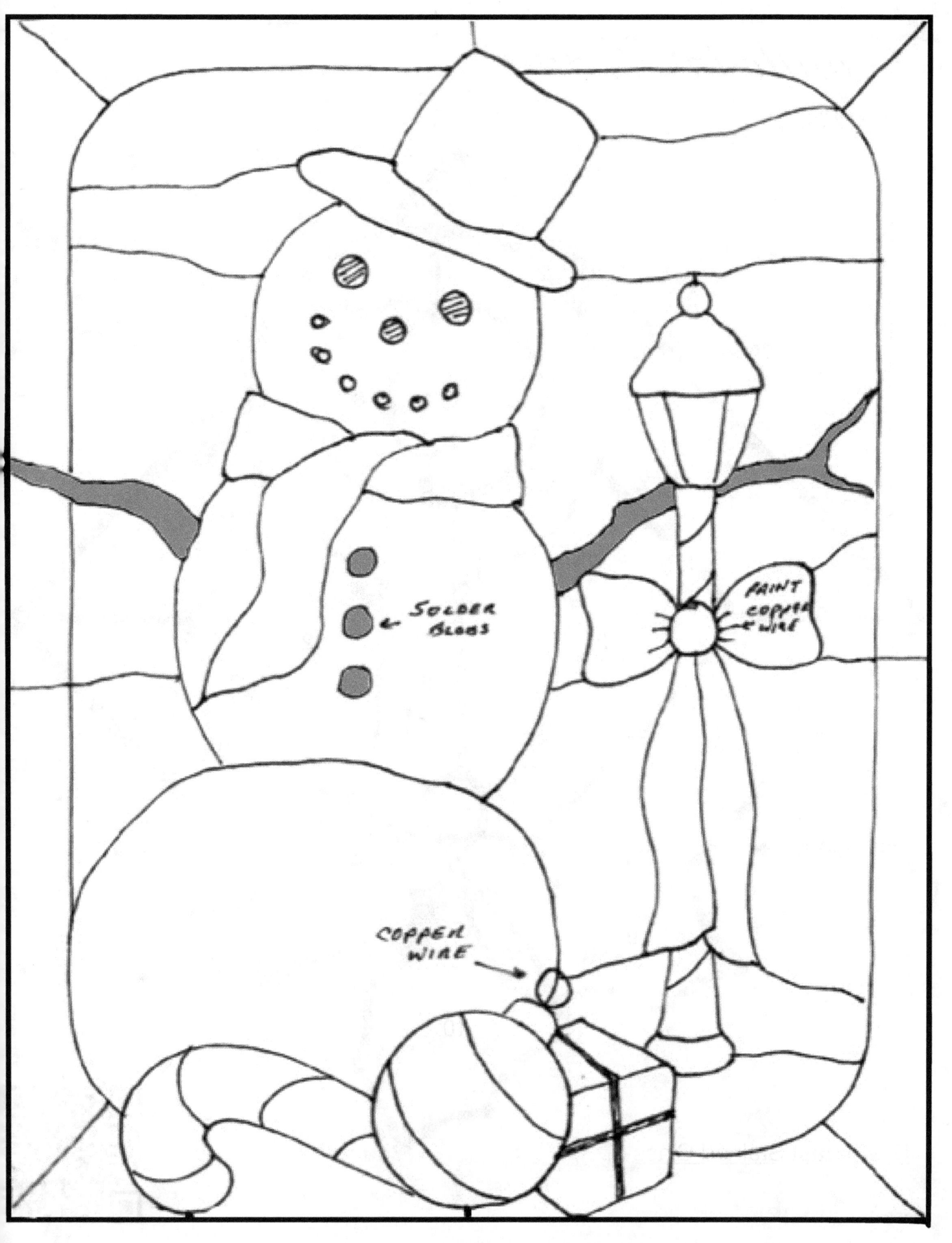

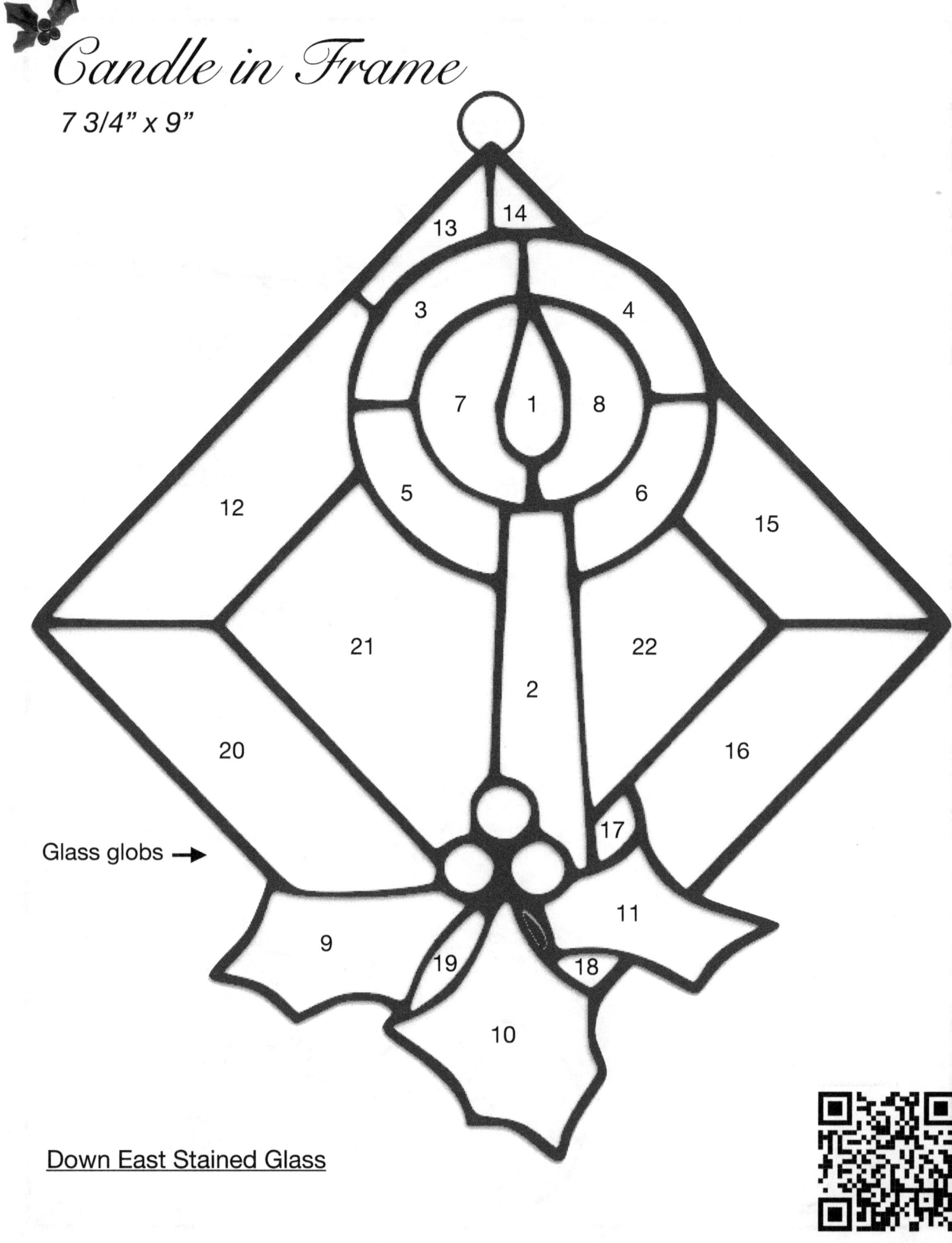

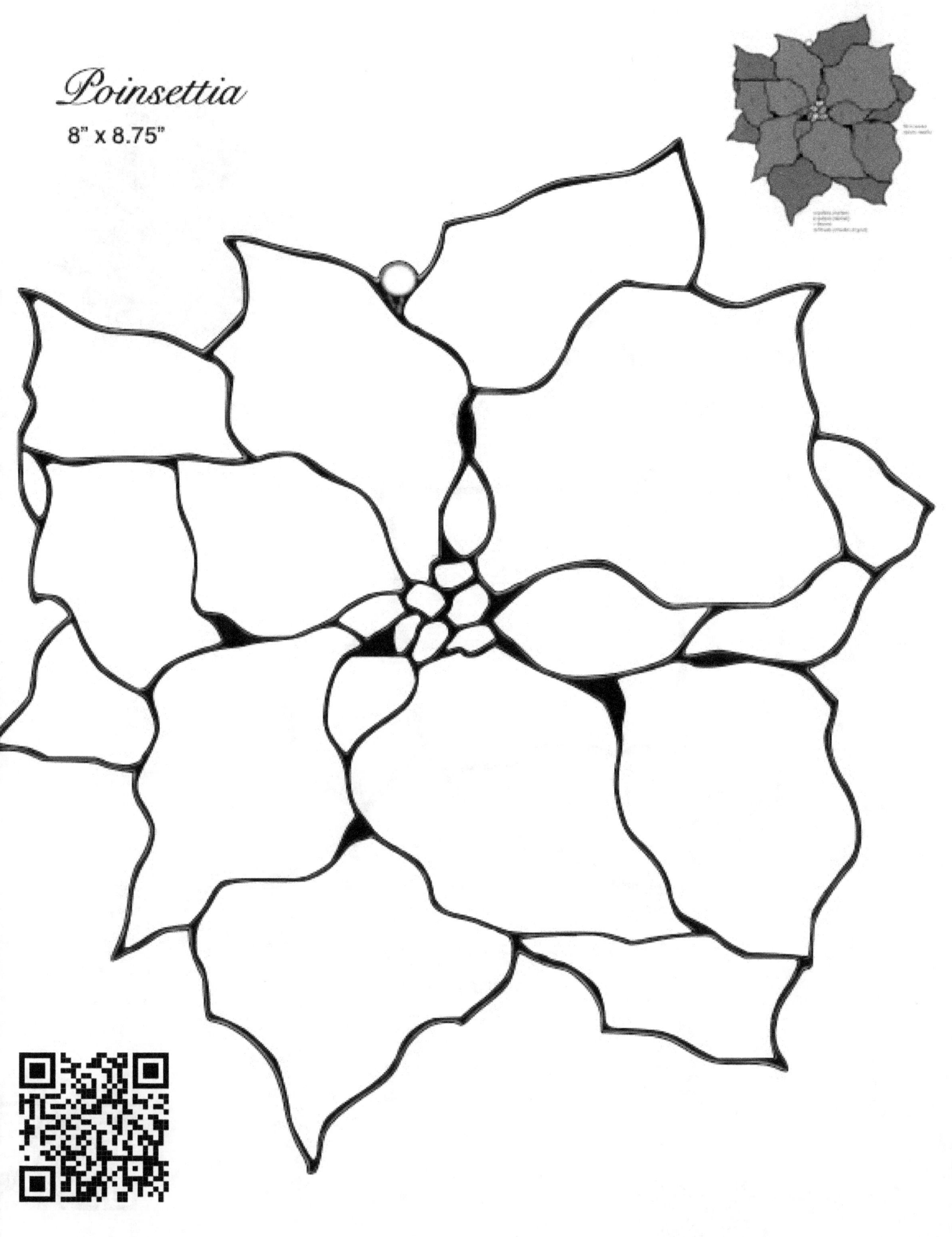

Poinsettia Spinner

Make 6 panels

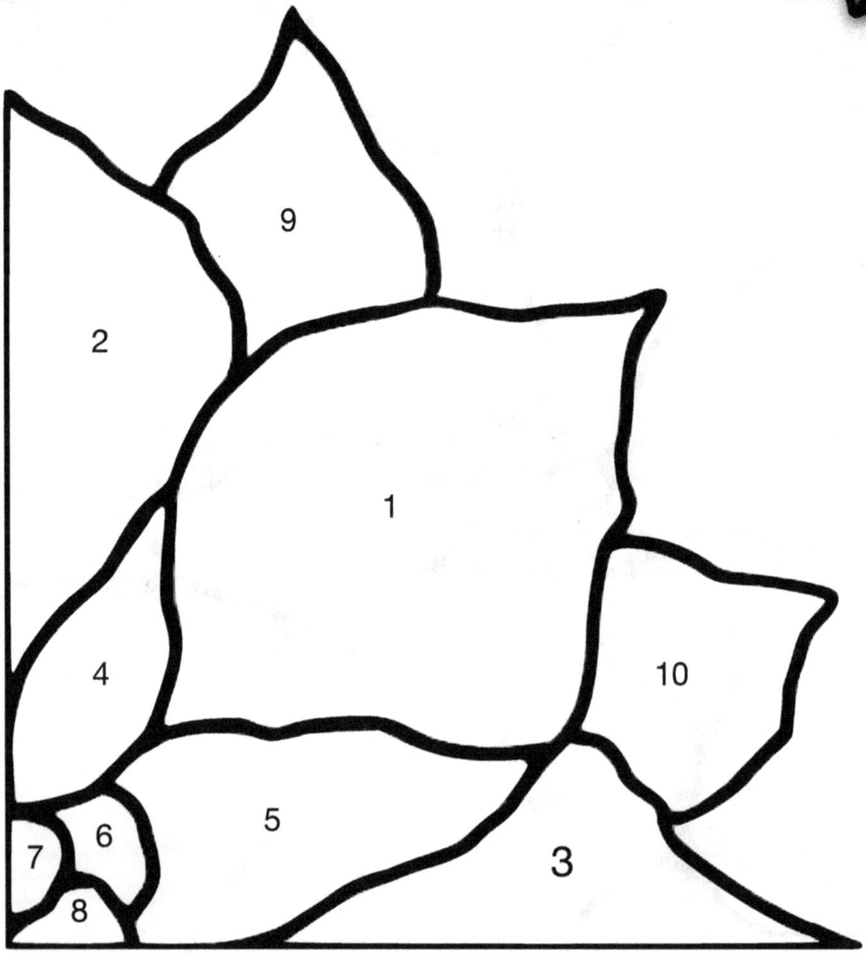

4 1/2" panels will make
9" spinner

Down East Stained Glass

Poinsettia Teardrop

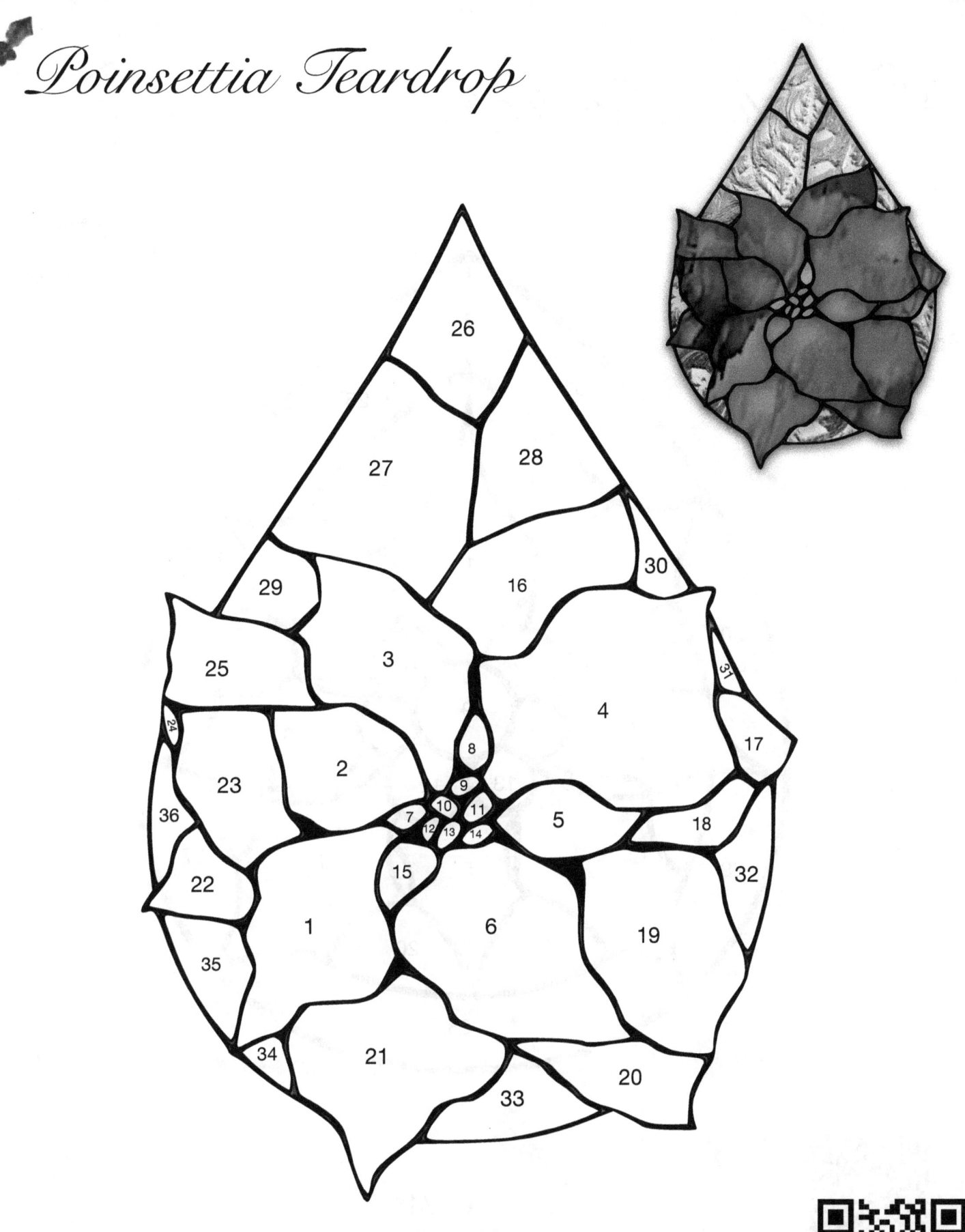

5" x 7.6"

Down East Stained Glass

Holly Teardrop

Spaces between leaves fill with solder

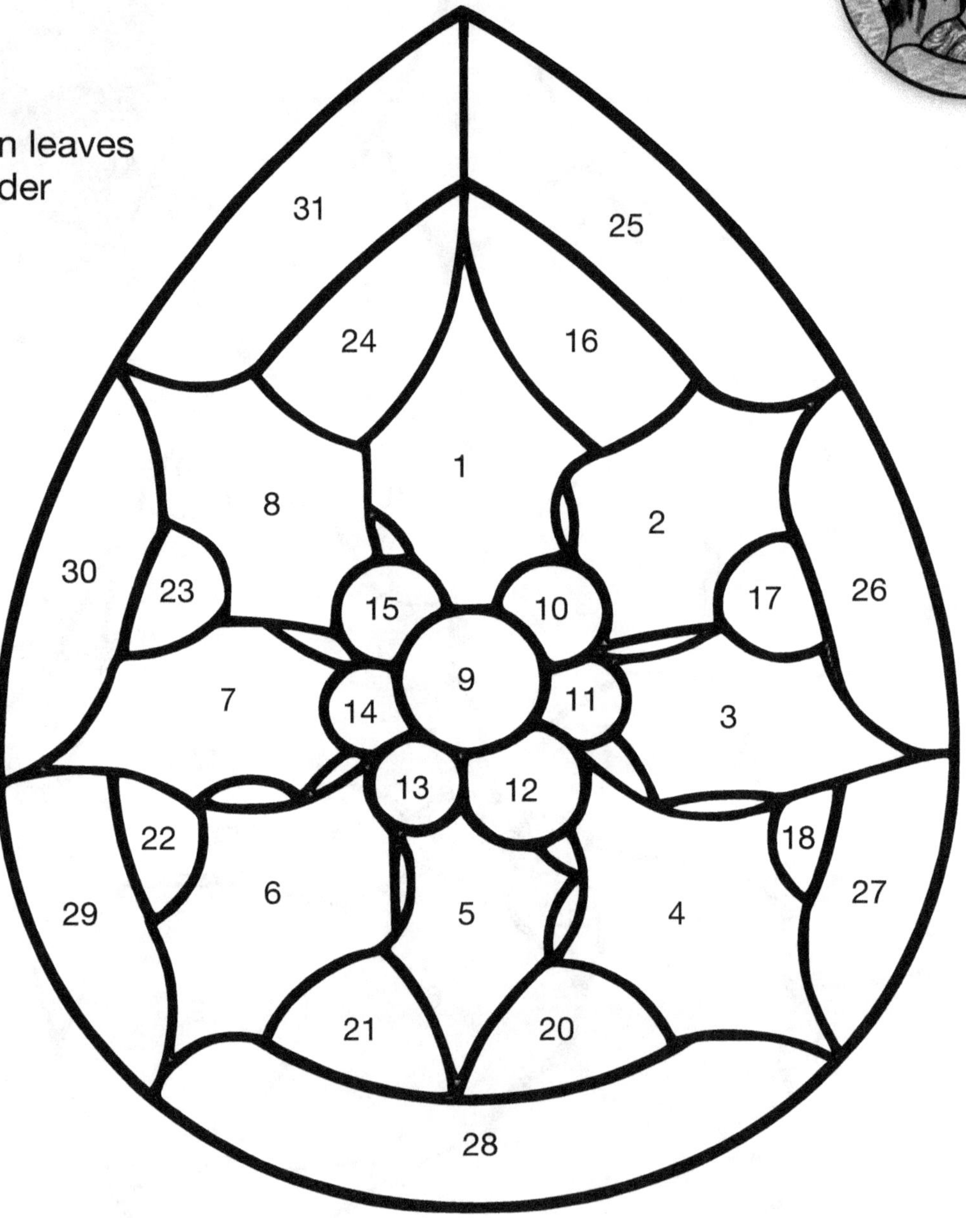

5" x 6 1/4"

Down East Stained Glass

Star of Bethlehem
5 1/2" x 7"

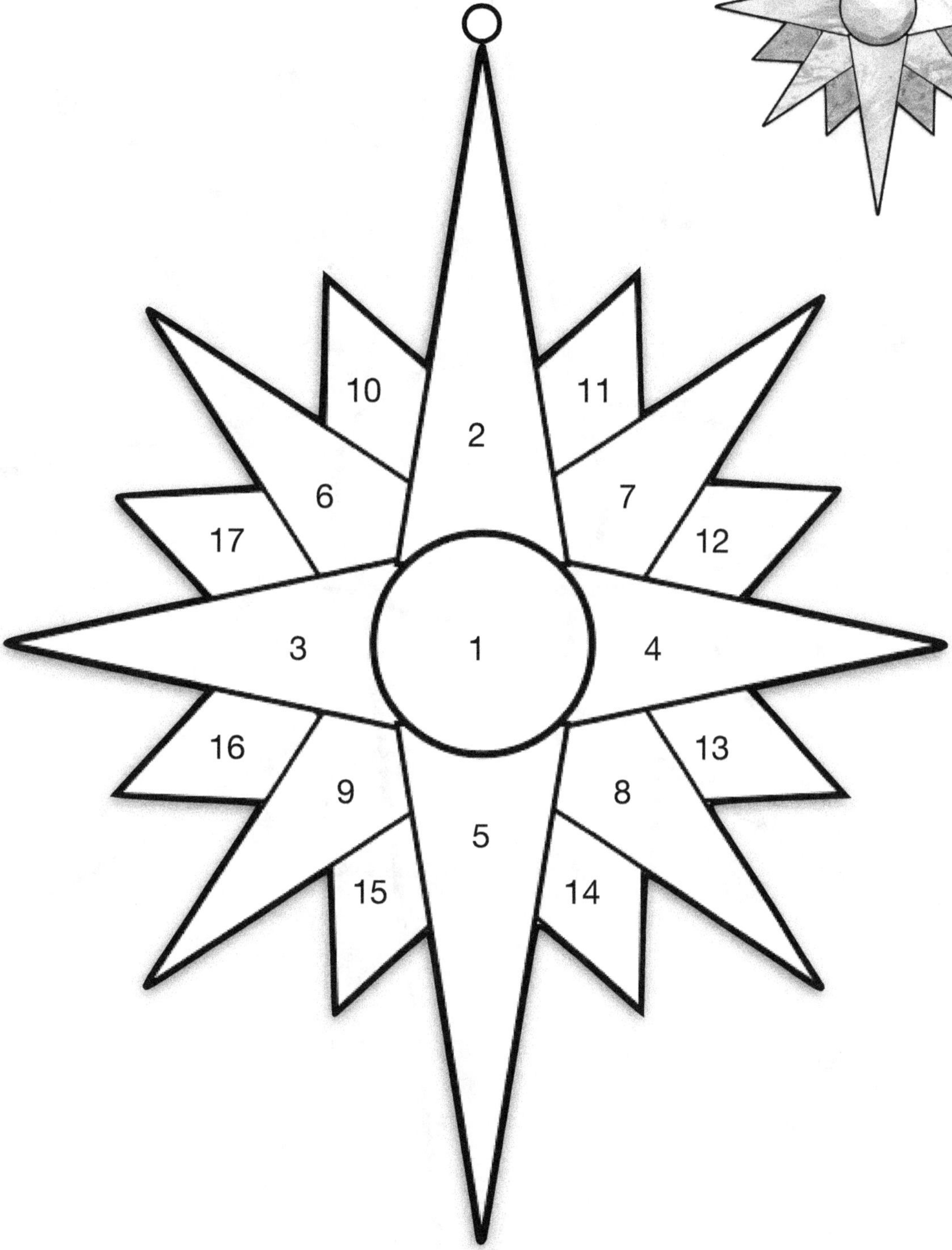

Down East Stained Glass

Star of Bethlehem 2
7" x 9.6"

Down East Stained Glass

Down East Christmas
Stained Glass Patterns

Gary Somers
©2025

www.ingramcontent.com/pod-product-compliance
Lightning Source LLC
Chambersburg PA
CBHW080443170426
43195CB00017B/2870